WISCONSIN CENTRAL

Railroad Success Story

Otto P. Dobnick and Steve Glischinski

WISCONSIN CENTRAL

Railroad Success Story

Otto P. Dobnick and Steve Glischinski

KALMBACH BOOKS

On the cover and page 2: Quite possibly the most popular train-watching location inherited by the Wisconsin Central from the old Soo Line was Byron Hill, the eastbound ruling grade on the Chicago Sub main line. On the crisp but cold afternoon of January 17, 1993, GP40 3000 is in charge of the tonnage making up this day's version of train T040, as it crests the hill 11 miles south of North Fond du Lac's Shops Yard heading for Chicago. The GP40 was part of a 17-unit acquisition in 1990 to bolster WC's ever-expanding Locomotive fleet. — *Otto P. Dobnick*

Published by Kalmbach Publishing Co., 21027 Crossroads Circle, Waukesha, WI 53187.

Printed in Hong Kong

97 98 99 00 01 02 03 04 05 06   10 9 8 7 6 5 4 3 2

Book design: Kristi Ludwig
Project editor: George Drury
Copy editor: Mary Algozin

Publisher's Cataloging in Publication
(Prepared by Quality Books Inc.)

Dobnick, Otto P.
        Wisconsin Central : railroad success story / Otto P. Dobnick and
Steve Glischinski.
        p.   cm.
        Includes index.
        ISBN 0-89024-562-2

        1. Wisconsin Central Railroad Company.   2. Railroads—United
States—History.   I. Glischinski, Steve.   I. Title.

TF25.W5D63 1996   385'.0973
                                QBI96-40464

CONTENTS

**Even the southernmost reaches of WC are not immune to winter's fury. SD45 6581 brings a westbound past
the tower and over the C&NW crossing at Deval Tower in Des Plaines, Ill., on January 30, 1994.** — *Ray Weart*

FOREWORD

Ten years ago, none of Wisconsin Central's founders ever dreamed they would be working for a new, entrepreneurial railroad. The possibility that they also would be railroading in four countries was as likely as the earth being flat.

The Wisconsin Central story, more than anything else, is a story of people. At the beginning virtually all of us, at all levels in the Company, were veterans of the Class 1 railroads. All we had known in our entire careers was downsizing and decay. We had witnessed the end of privately operated passenger service, the abandonment of thousands of miles of branch line, the elimination of hundreds of thousands of railroad jobs, and bankruptcies. We had seen trucks become the primary mode of freight transportation, while railroads were reduced to handling low-value bulk traffic, where service was secondary. After all, we were told, railroads cannot provide good service at a price our customers can afford.

The decision by the Soo Line in late 1986 to put its Lake States Division up for sale was a recognition on its part that those lines were dead or dying. Many thought Soo Line's action was a calculated plan to avoid having to

Edward A. Burkhardt — *Photo by Pete Briggs*

abandon these lines, leaving them to waste away at the hands of undercapitalized shortline railroaders instead.

But a small core of businessmen saw opportunity where Soo Line had failed, and soon they were to be joined by hundreds of railroad people who shared a simple formula for success: keep costs down and customer service up, be competitive, be productive, and maintain the property.

Wisconsin Central almost did not make it through its first six months, but employee teamwork saved the day. We have not looked back. Our success in a market characterized by low traffic density, a preponderance of single car shipments, and cutthroat motor carrier competition is now legendary. But we had several important factors going for us, notably our employees and our customers.

I cannot say enough about the employees who have made Wisconsin Central what it is. These people, primarily veterans of Class 1 railroads, put their shoulders to the wheel and have never stopped. Countless predictions had been made that the poor attitudes and weak work ethic all too often found on Class 1s would follow these workers to the Wisconsin Central. These predictions were wrong.

Many railroaders who came to Wisconsin Central had lost their jobs on the Class 1s, and they were determined to make WC a success. In my opinion, there are no better employee attitudes and work ethic among railroaders than those found on Wisconsin Central.

WC's customer list is a dream come true. Just as we are blessed with the best employees, no railroad has a better, more loyal customer group than WC. Our shippers provide strong backing for "their railroad" whenever we need them, and we have been lucky to participate in their growth. Perhaps we have had something to do with that growth, which is the way it's supposed to be! All our shippers want is a fair price, good service, and good equipment. That is not rocket science, but these ideas seem revolutionary in our industry. And if you meet these demands, wonderful things happen to your business.

Wisconsin Central has saved thousands of miles of railroad from the scrapper's torch, instead turning them into a great success story. We have created and preserved about 2,000 permanent, family-supporting jobs. We have generated a solid return for the stockholders who risked their money in markets where others were retreating. It has been a pleasure to work with this committed team of railroad men and women.

Our ventures in New Zealand, Canada, and the United Kingdom have brought us in contact with excellent railroaders who share the values we hold dear. All the organizations have benefited from exchanges of technology, ideas, and personnel. I have been particularly impressed with our friends at Tranz Rail in New Zealand. These people run an excellent railroad, and we have as much to learn from them as they have to learn from us.

I have high hopes for our venture in Britain. It must be some form of manifest destiny that we are going back to the place where our industry was born, to spread the message of productivity, competitiveness, and customer service. I think the next eight years will be just as interesting and productive as the years have been since that shaky start in 1987.

Business people are poor historians. They are busy creating history in their fields and rarely have time to document it. I appreciate the willingness of the authors to take on the task of telling the Wisconsin Central story.

Edward A. Burkhardt
President, Wisconsin Central Transportation Corp.
Rosemont, Illinois

INTRODUCTION AND ACKNOWLEDGMENTS

The book you are about to read makes no secret of the fact that Wisconsin Central has brought rapid and far-reaching changes to the railroad picture in the upper Midwest. The scene has been changing so quickly that possibly the greatest challenge faced by the authors was deciding where to end the manuscript, knowing that additional trains, line acquisitions, and other operating ideas were on the horizon even as the book went to press. We knew that WC would wait for no author. Yet the eve of WC's tenth birthday seemed the right time to chronicle the dynamic events of Wisconsin Central's first decade. As other facets of WC history unfold, so may the need for a subsequent volume to continue the story. We trust you will find its story as interesting to explore as we have.

Recognition is in order for those who assisted us with the many details of putting together this book, including checking facts, reviewing and proofreading the manuscript, providing photographs, and assisting in production efforts. We were assisted by numerous enthusiastic WC employees, including many who were involved in the start-up and growth of the company. It is impossible to name everyone, but special thanks go to Edward A. Burkhardt, Alex A. Amundson, Brian R. Buchanan, John W. Carey, Paul Enenbach, James E. Fisk, Barry O. Karlberg, Timothy M. Kelly, Glenn J. Kerbs, Barbara A. Lane, John Leopard, Robert F. Nadrowski, Charles W. Newton, William R. Schauer, Richard F. Soyk, and David A. Wilson. We truly appreciate their help and also their pride in their railroad.

Many others also helped and supported us in one way or another: Nancy M. Anderson, Robert C. Anderson, Bud Bulgrin, Bill Christopher, Mike Cleary, Jeff Hampton, Fred Hyde, and Lori Van Oosbree. Special thanks go to Peter A. Briggs for answering countless questions and making many important suggestions; J. David Ingles for his assistance with the manuscript and his enthusiasm for the project; and George H. Drury of Kalmbach Books for shepherding this project to completion.

Finally, there's the multitude of photographers whose talents we were privileged to utilize to illustrate this story. Selecting the photos from the thousands of excellent images available was difficult — little escapes the viewfinders of WC's trackside photographers. We also thank those whose work we couldn't use because of space limitations. We appreciate their efforts, talents, and patience.

Otto P. Dobnick
Waukesha, Wisconsin
November, 1996

Steve Glischinski
Shoreview, Minnesota
November, 1996

Soo train 944 crosses the massive St. Croix River Bridge and enters the Badger State near Somerset, Wis., on October 2, 1976, behind F7A 2227B and two SD40-2s. The train was handed off by Canadian Pacific to Soo at Portal, N.D., the day before and is bound for Soo's Schiller Park Yard near Chicago. The St. Croix bridge, the largest on the Soo Line, stretches 2,682 feet between abutments, and its single track is 185 feet above the river. Five steel arches, each spanning 350 feet, make up the main spans; the remainder is of steel viaduct construction. The steelwork was built by American Bridge Co. and erected by Kelly Atkinson Construction Co. of Chicago. It includes 5,035 tons of structural steel and cost more than a half million 1910 dollars, but allowed the abandonment of tortuous grades that took the old main line down to a 10-span deck truss bridge only 100 feet above water level. The first train crossed the bridge on June 3, 1911. In 1987 it would become Wisconsin Central property. — *Steve Glischinski*

1

A RICH HERITAGE

WISCONSIN CENTRAL'S PREDECESSORS

The Wisconsin Central of the 1990s is a thoroughly modern, progressive regional railroad serving Illinois, Michigan, Minnesota, Wisconsin, and the Canadian province of Ontario with over 2,800 miles of track. When WC was formed in 1987, its system encompassed trackage from several well-known predecessor railroads including the Chicago, Milwaukee, St. Paul & Pacific, the Duluth, South Shore & Atlantic, and the Minneapolis, St. Paul & Sault Ste. Marie. However, most of WC's trackage in Wisconsin is descended from the original Wisconsin Central, a railroad born in the 19th century.

The Wisconsin Central Railway was incorporated on February 4, 1871, to tap the rich natural resources of the Badger State. At the time, the federal government was offering land grants to railroads to entice them to build into unsettled regions. One such grant was for lands and adjacent timber areas on a route from central Wisconsin to Lake Superior. To take advantage of this grant, on June

The original WC used its trademark shield on just about everything, including locomotives, stationery, tickets, and even switchstands. A handful of these switchstands survived into the "new" WC era, as exemplified by this one at the Ashland yard in 1987.
— *Otto P. Dobnick*

15, 1871, ground for the WC was broken at West Menasha (now Neenah) for a line to Stevens Point (it would eventually reach Ashland). The 63-mile line to "Point" was completed in only 153 days, with the first train arriving on November 15. The WC reached Ashland in 1877 and was granted nearly a million acres of land for completing the line.

The Wolf River played a vital part in the development of Waupaca County between Neenah and Stevens Point. The river was also a barrier to the original Wisconsin Central, which had to construct a bridge when building west from Menasha in 1871. At Gill's Landing, just east of the community of Weyauwega, a train of the turn-of-the-century Wisconsin Central poses on the Wolf River drawbridge behind 4-4-0 No. 100. Note the WC "shield" numberplate on the locomotive. This emblem, adapted from a shield in the coat of arms of the great seal of the state of Wisconsin, was adopted by WC in 1885. — *Collection of Russ Porter*

Wisconsin Central 4-4-0 No. 87 stands in Chicago's Grand Central Station about 1895. Engineer Jim Glover is leaning on the main rod, and fireman Bob McClure stands next to the pilot beam. — *State Historical Society of Wisconsin, negative WHi (X3) 24516*

Shield-shaped paddles serve as markers at the rear of a Wisconsin Central caboose at Wheeler, Wisconsin, about 1907. — *State Historical Society of Wisconsin, negative WHi (X3) 50553*

This was not the first time the name "Wisconsin Central" had been used nor the last. In 1853 a Wisconsin Central was chartered to build from Chicago to the west end of Lake Superior. The company started work and laid some track in 1855 and 1856 between McHenry, Illinois, and Genoa City, Wisconsin. It graded right-of-way in Wisconsin to Lake Geneva and as far as Jefferson. The line south of Lake Geneva ultimately became part of Chicago & North Western.

In 1980 another Wisconsin Central briefly appeared as a new short line taking over operation of an ex-Milwaukee Road branch between Waukesha and Milton, Wis. Because of property titles and securities still tied to the pre-1961 Wisconsin Central, however, the Interstate Commerce Commission (ICC) ordered the short line to change its name. It became the Central Wisconsin Railroad. In 1996 this line was being operated by Wisconsin & Southern Railroad.

The WC of 1871 expanded rapidly. In 1876 it constructed a branch from Stevens Point to Portage; most of this line was abandoned in 1945. WC reached St. Paul in 1884, arrived at Chicago in 1886, and built a branch from Mellen to Hurley to reach the Gogebic Iron Range in 1887. A branch from Menasha to Manitowoc was completed in 1896, and WC finally reached Superior in 1908. It reached Milwaukee by trackage rights on the Milwaukee Road from a connection at Rugby Junction, south of what is now Slinger.

In 1885 WC adopted a shield as its trademark. The shield came from the coat of arms on the great seal of the

Bridging the Baltimore River at Bruce Crossing, Mich., ex-DSS&A Baldwin AS-616s 204 and 210 have a freight well in hand as they head east on September 3, 1961. The new Soo Line Railroad Company is only nine months old, but it's apparent that mechanical department forces haven't had time to focus on repainting locomotives. The "new Soo" would continue to route Marquette-Ashland freights along the old South Shore into the late 1970s, when operations dwindled to "as needed." WC would run only a handful of trains — all bound for White Pine mine — through Bruce Crossing before tearing up the Sidnaw-Bergland portion of the DSS&A in 1989. — *Robert C. Anderson*

Passengers disembark from DSS&A's Budd RDC, the Shoreliner, in Marquette, Mich., on a cold day in the late 1950s. The car ran less than three years for the South Shore before it was sold to Canadian Pacific in 1959. The car was conveyed to VIA, Canada's national passenger railroad, in 1978 and remained in service into the 1990s, one of the last pieces of South Shore equipment still in operation. — *Gordon De Haas*

The original Wisconsin Central opened its shops in Waukesha, Wis., in 1887, but they remained in operation for little more than a decade, closing in 1900. The buildings survived into the 1980s. On April 12, 1987, the old shop building shows off its raised stone Wisconsin Central name. — *Otto P. Dobnick*

On June 21, 1959, 4-6-2 No. 2719 closed out steam operations on the Soo Line when it pulled an excursion sponsored by the Minnesota Railfans Association from Minneapolis to Ladysmith, Wis., and return. For the trip, Soo was able to coax the Interstate Commerce Commission into granting one final flue extension for the 2719. (Boiler flues had to be replaced at regular intervals, but extensions could be granted if the locomotive had not been in continuous active service.) Engine 2719 is taking on coal and water at Dresser, Wis., illuminated by a short burst of sunshine during a day of otherwise gloomy weather. The Pacific was saved and placed in a park in Eau Claire, Wis., where it is currently the subject of restoration efforts. — *Robert C. Anderson*

state of Wisconsin. James Barker, WC's General Passenger and Ticket Agent, described the reason for using the shield in an 1885 letter: "The home of the Wisconsin Central being in Wisconsin, the idea suggested itself to make use of some form that would at once be recognized as appropriate." WC used it on cars, locomotives, and even switch stands. A century later the same shield would also be adopted by the new Wisconsin Central.

The WC's work was cut out for it. Many of its lines were constructed after other railroads had already been spiked down through Wisconsin. While WC persevered, it always seemed to be an also-ran: its routes were longer, and it found itself the second railroad in many communities. In 1889 the transcontinental Northern Pacific contracted with WC to operate through train service for it from the Twin Cities to Chicago, and the following year NP leased the WC. In 1893, however, NP entered receivership and defaulted on its lease payments to WC, effectively ending its control.

Between 1887 and 1897, WC operated commuter train service between Chicago and suburban River Forest. Although the service soon vanished, 100 years later Metra, Chicago's commuter railroad, would revive suburban operations on the new WC.

For the early WC, the period from 1893 to 1909 was one of improvement. The railroad upgraded its lines and raised them out of the marshy lands with tons of rock ballast. WC moved its shops from Waukesha to larger facilities in North Fond du Lac. It constructed new depots, and traffic was on the increase as Wisconsin industry prospered — but the road remained financially troubled.

WC's salvation would come in the form of an alliance with the Minneapolis, St. Paul & Sault Ste. Marie (Soo Line), which had been incorporated on September 29, 1883, as the Minneapolis, St. Paul & Atlantic Railway. The MStP&A was the brainchild of Minneapolis milling interests, who were anxious to find a way to ship their product east without going through time-consuming and expensive interchanges in Chicago. Their answer was to bypass Chicago by building a 493-mile line direct from Minneapolis to a connection with Canadian Pacific at Sault Ste. Marie, Ontario.

Construction of this line began in April 1884 at Cameron, Wis., and the line reached Sault Ste. Marie in December 1887. Originally the road got into Minneapolis by trackage rights from Turtle Lake, Wis., over the Chicago, St. Paul, Minneapolis & Omaha ("Omaha Road"). This situation was remedied when a MStP&A subsidiary, the Minneapolis & St. Croix Railway, was constructed from Turtle Lake to Minneapolis. The new through Minneapolis-Sault Ste. Marie route opened for business in January 1888.

At the same time, the Minneapolis interests incorporated the Minneapolis & Pacific Railway to build west of the Twin Cities to bring wheat from the Dakotas to Minneapolis. Like so many railroad ventures of the era, all three railroad companies encountered financial problems, but Canadian Pacific stepped in to prop them up, mandating that they be consolidated. This began a long relationship with the Canadian carrier. On June 11, 1888, the three railroads were united to form the Minneapolis, St. Paul & Sault Ste. Marie Railway, nicknamed "Soo Line." "Soo" is the pronunciation of Sault, and the twin Michigan and Ontario cities of Sault Ste. Marie, the line's eastern gateway, are locally called "the Soo" — hence the railroad's nickname.

Soo Line recognized the value of the WC and in 1908 acquired a majority stock interest, then leased the entire railroad on April 1, 1909. Under the agreement, WC remained a separate entity and the Soo did not participate in its profits or losses or pay any rent for the property. However, together the two roads gained traffic from each other and Soo garnered access to Chicago. To the general public, it was all Soo Line. But to railroaders, WC continued a separate existence with its own offices, company officers, and stockholders. WC steam locomotives were numbered with four digits, and carried small WC initials on the cab. This practice continued into the diesel era, with units numbered in four-digit series and small WC initials on the carbody or cab. WC even built its own diesel shop in 1955 at North Fond du Lac, which 32 years later would become home shop for the new Wisconsin Central. The original WC would remain a ward of the Soo for 52 years, although the lease agreement ended in 1932 with WC's bankruptcy. After 1932 Soo acted as WC's "operating agent."

Another line whose track would become part of the new Wisconsin Central was the Wisconsin & Northern Railroad. Incorporated in 1906, the W&N built a line from Neenah to W&N Junction, near Argonne. It was purchased by Soo Line in 1921.

One of WC's more colorful predecessors was the Duluth, South Shore & Atlantic Railway, based at Marquette on Michigan's upper peninsula. The South Shore was incorporated in 1887 as a consolidation of several railroads serving Michigan's iron-ore country. DSS&A's stated purpose and ultimate achievement was to build a railroad from the Twin Ports of Duluth and Superior to Sault Ste. Marie. Branches were added to Houghton-Hancock, on Michigan's copper-rich Keweenaw Peninsula, and to St. Ignace, on the Straits of Mackinac. From there, carferry service connected South Shore trains with Michigan's lower peninsula. DSS&A eventually reached deeper into the copper country of the Keweenaw when it acquired control of the Mineral Range Railroad, which operated north from Hancock. DSS&A came under Canadian Pacific control in 1890.

The South Shore was intended in part to be a major iron-ore hauler, but when the Lake Superior & Ishpeming arrived on the Marquette iron range in 1896, it cut into much of DSS&A's business. Nonetheless, South Shore maintained large ore docks on the Marquette waterfront and in 1931 opened a 900-foot concrete structure. The ore business finally played out in 1971, and the dock has sat unused for the last 26 years. Never an especially prosperous carrier, the South Shore filed for bankruptcy in 1937, emerging in 1949 as the Duluth, South Shore & Atlantic Railroad. At the same time, DSS&A formally merged its subsidiary Mineral Range Railroad.

On December 31, 1960, the Duluth, South Shore & Atlantic, the Minneapolis, St. Paul & Sault Ste. Marie, and the Wisconsin Central were merged. Referred to as the "New Soo," the new company was formed using the DSS&A corporate structure. So at merger it was actually the DSS&A that survived, with its name changed to Soo Line Railroad Company. Most of the "New Soo" lines in Wisconsin and all of its Michigan trackage would become a part of the new Wisconsin Central

Two lines of the Chicago, Milwaukee, St. Paul & Pacific (The Milwaukee Road) would be included in the new WC: the Valley line from New Lisbon to Tomahawk and part of the old Superior Division main line from

In the early 1970s the north end of Milwaukee Road's "Valley Line" between Wausau and Heafford Junction was worked by trains 263 and 272. No. 263 worked north and set out cars at Merrill, interchanged with the Marinette, Tomahawk & Western at Tomahawk, and exchanged cars with Soo at Heafford Junction. Returning south in September 1974, train 272 meanders through Merrill behind an Alco RSD-5 and an F unit. The Valley Line was an Alco haven until the units were retired in spring 1976. — *Terry Norton*

Pride of the Soo Line from 1951 to 1965 was the Chicago-Duluth/Superior *Laker*. While other roads spent millions to purchase streamlined passenger cars after World War II, Soo was content to rebuild its old heavy-weight cars and concentrate on good service. The service, begun in 1951, lasted only 14 years. On July 25, 1962 the *Laker*, heavy with head-end traffic, makes its station stop at Forest Park, Ill. Three WC boiler-equipped GP9s, 2555, 2552, and 2553, are on the point. Two of the three, 2553 and 2555, would still be going strong for CP Rail's Soo Line in 1996 — more than 40 years after they were built. —*J. David Ingles*

Canco, a junction in northern Milwaukee, to Green Bay. The 133-mile Valley line (named for the Wisconsin River valley, which it follows), was constructed in several parts between 1871 and 1895. The Milwaukee-Green Bay route was built by the Milwaukee & Northern from 1870 to 1873. In 1893 the Chicago, Milwaukee & St. Paul (the "Pacific" was not added to its name until 1928) acquired the Milwaukee & Northern, which continued north of Green Bay into the upper peninsula of Michigan. Both the Valley and Green Bay lines remained in Milwaukee Road hands until the entire railroad was sold to Soo Line in 1985. Ultimately, part or all of several other Midwestern railroads would also be folded into WC.

THE CLASSIC YEARS

The 15 years from the end of World War II to the Soo Line merger could easily be tabbed the "classic years" of WC's predecessor lines. During this colorful period, the transition was made from steam to diesel motive power, passenger services were upgraded, and freight traffic volume rose as the physical plant was overhauled to handle more traffic. Many people fondly remember railroading in WC territory in the postwar years, with time freights, iron ore, pulpwood, and passengers moving across the system.

With the end of the war in 1945, dieselization ended the reign of two handsome classes of WC steam power: the N-20 class 4-8-2 Mountain type and the O-20 4-8-4 Northerns. Three of the 21 4-8-2s were built by Shoreham Shops in Minneapolis in 1929 and 1930 with boilers provided by American Locomotive Company. The four 4-8-4s were the largest steam locomotives on the old WC. Delivered in 1938 by Lima Locomotive Works, they were so large they were restricted to main lines.

Regular service steam finished on WC when 2-8-0 No. 468 ran into the roundhouse at Neenah on February 15, 1955. The very last steam locomotive to run on the Soo Line was WC 4-6-2 2719, which pulled a Minnesota Railfans Association excursion from Minneapolis to Ladysmith, Wis., and return on June 21, 1959.

Taking the place of steam in Soo road service were handsome, streamlined EMD F3 and F7 diesels and Alco FA freight units. The first F3s arrived in 1947 wearing an attractive — if conservative — maroon and gold paint scheme. The colors were eventually applied to almost all road diesels but were especially well suited to the cab units on whose nose was a squared-off gold "pine tree" outlined in black. A variation of this scheme would be adopted by the new Wisconsin Central.

The South Shore was the first WC predecessor to dieselize completely. The railroad endeared itself to trainwatchers by dieselizing with American Locomotive (Alco) and Baldwin products — and by attiring them in another attractive paint scheme, yellow and green with Chinese red trim. DSS&A's later steam power mainly consisted of 4-6-0s, 2-8-0s, 4-6-2s, and secondhand 2-8-2s. The last DSS&A steam run was made in 1954.

Alco road switchers dieselized Milwaukee Road's Valley line in 1947, and diesels took over from steam on the Green Bay line in 1950 and 1951.

While no DSS&A steam locomotives survived, Soo Line did preserve a number of engines, at least nine of which are on display in cities served by Wisconsin Central Ltd. Few Milwaukee engines escaped scrap, but one large survivor, 4-8-4 No. 261, was donated to the National Railroad Museum in Green Bay. It was restored to service in 1993 and pulled several excursions on WC.

While most railroads invested heavily in streamlined passenger equipment after the war, Soo Line stuck with heavyweight rolling stock, painted wine red with gold lettering. On June 3, 1951, the *Laker* began operation between Chicago (on Lake Michigan) and Duluth and Superior (at the head of the Great Lakes). The new train was introduced with ads that tweaked streamliners of the neighboring roads by proclaiming, "Soo improves where it counts — INSIDE — where you ride." Connecting trains operated from Spencer to Ashland and from Owen to the Twin Cities. Highway and air competition resulted in the end of the *Laker* on January 16, 1965.

Passenger service was never a big item on DSS&A's balance sheet, but in 1955 the railroad made a last attempt to draw passengers by purchasing a Budd Rail Diesel Car (RDC). Dubbed the *Shoreliner*, the car operated only three years before local passenger service was discontinued and the RDC sent to parent Canadian Pacific. DSS&A, in cooperation with Milwaukee Road, also operated the famous *Copper Country Limited* between Chicago and Calumet, Mich. Inaugurated in 1907, the train kept rolling until March 8, 1968, the last pure passenger operation on the Soo. The Soo permitted passengers to ride cabooses on certain trains in Wisconsin and Upper Michigan until September 1986.

In addition to the *Copper Country Limited,* other Milwaukee Road "name" trains plied routes that are part of today's Wisconsin Central. The *Chippewa-Hiawatha* ran between Chicago and Ontonagon, Mich., using the line now operated by WC between Milwaukee and Green Bay, and the *North Woods Hiawatha* used the Wisconsin River "Valley Line." A remnant of this train remained in operation until October 7, 1970, the last pure passenger train to operate over what would become the WC system in 1987.

The period following World War II was also an era of personalized freight service, with railroads handling much less-than-carload freight (LCL). Towns large and small had depots manned by friendly agents who would personally take care of your shipping or travel needs. In some cases the agents even lived in the depot. The idea of personal service gave way as communication technology advanced. Depots closed and agencies were consolidated to a central location, but the new Wisconsin Central would revive the idea of personal customer service, albeit by telephone, computer, and fax machine.

CHANGING TIMES

With dieselization, the "new Soo" merger, the end of passenger service, and a frugal management, the Soo Line of the 1960s and 1970s was a profitable railroad. Despite being surrounded by larger rail and truck competitors, it continued to turn a profit, relying on healthy grain business and traffic levels to and from the United States for parent Canadian Pacific. Soo Line invested heavily in its physical plant, installing welded rail on main lines and grain branches alike, expanding CTC signal coverage in Illinois, Minnesota, and Wisconsin, and purchasing new locomotives and cars.

For nearly two decades Soo was led by former DSS&A President Leonard H. Murray. Known for his frugality, Murray took the helm at merger and held it until 1978, when he moved up to chairman and CEO. Murray can be credited with continually improving Soo's revenues, while controlling costs and increasing traffic — he was a master of using the minimal resources at his disposal. He was followed in the president's chair by fellow DSS&A'er

Charging east on Soo's Minneapolis-Stevens Point main line, train 944 is about to split the community of Cylon, Wis., on September 6, 1976. Up front are SD40s 752 and 739 and SD40-2 789. The three SDs represent typical Soo mainline power of the 1970s: between 1969 and 1984 the road purchased 78 examples of the SD40 and the SD40-2. — *Steve Glischinski*

Entering Shoreham Yard in Minneapolis, a westbound Soo time freight is about to complete its trip from Chippewa Falls on June 1, 1968. Middle unit in the consist is two-month old U30C 800. The ten 3,000-horse-power "U-boats" purchased by Soo were never held in high regard, being the only GE diesels on a mostly EMD roster. They were also vastly outperformed by EMD's popular SD40, which Soo began buying in quantity in 1969. Stored in their later years, the U30Cs were sold and scrapped in 1983 and 1984. — *J. David Ingles*

Tom Beckley. In 1983 Dennis Cavanaugh took over the reins of the Soo.

The situation Cavanaugh faced in 1983 was considerably different from that which Murray faced in 1961. Murray and company had built the Soo into a strong property, which in 1980 produced 3 percent of the entire rail industry's pretax net profit — on only 2.5 percent of the total Class 1 rail mileage. The gradual collapse of the Milwaukee Road and the Rock Island in the late 1970s gave Soo more business, as did C&NW's withering service to Wisconsin rail customers. Several competitors went out of existence when they merged with other railroads. Deregulation of the rail industry under the Staggers Act of 1980 finally freed railroads from cumbersome government regulations under which they had chafed for nearly a century, allowing railroads to negotiate long-term contracts and adjust rates. In most respects, the Soo that Cavanaugh inherited was doing well.

In others, though, Soo had some catching up to do. While its track was good, the railroad held trains to a maximum of 40 mph systemwide — a speed hardly conducive to outdoing rail or truck competitors. Another concern was labor costs. Even as other railroads aggressively negotiated labor agreements that included reductions in the size of train crews, Soo didn't make a move until the late 1980s. Even in 1994, some Soo Line trains still operated with four-person crews, long after competing railroads were using two crew members on most trains. In many instances crew districts were short, usually 100 miles or so, a holdover from the steam era. It took four crews to move a Soo Line train from Minneapolis to Chicago, while Burlington Northern managed to reduce to two crews over its route.

Railroading in the Soo Line's region continued to change with the deregulation not only of railroads but also trucking, the decline of heavy industry, and loss of local business. Soo was becoming a small railroad in a land of giants. Other railroads were expanding or merging to increase market share, but the Soo was content to continue its conservative but profitable ways.

Even before the Cavanaugh regime, though, Soo decided that to survive in the long term, it had to expand its traffic mix and reach new gateways to obtain longer hauls and larger market share. Kansas City was a logical target, since it offered a longer haul and connections to virtually every major western system. Soo made an aggressive move to purchase Rock Island's "Spine Line" between the Twin Cities and Kansas City. It even acquired the 45-mile Minneapolis, Northfield & Southern in January 1982, which connected with the Spine Line in Northfield, Minn. — but the Spine Line went instead to Chicago & North Western.

Failing in that bid, Soo instead put all its resources into trying to purchase the Milwaukee Road, which had cut back to a 3,100-mile, midwest-only rail system in 1980, following its 1977 bankruptcy. Through its Grand Trunk Western subsidiary, Canadian National Railways was pursuing the Milwaukee Road, but then C&NW, with deeper pockets, entered the fray. The battle soon grew too rich for CN, and it appeared as though Soo would again lose to C&NW, since the latter offered to buy the Milwaukee for $786 million versus Soo's $575 million. But on February 9, 1985, U. S. District Court Judge Thomas R. McMillen, who was handling Milwaukee's bankruptcy case, shocked the railroad world by awarding the Milwaukee Road to the Soo, the second-highest bidder. McMillen cited the fact that Soo's bid was more in line with the public interest, in part because Soo would not abandon any lines. C&NW, confident of victory and with a merger plan ready, had promised abandonments of 1,000 miles or so of parallel trackage. On February 19 Soo Line expanded from a 4400-mile railroad to a 7,500-mile system, stretching from the Canadian border to Louisville and Kansas City.

C&NW, knowing it had overbid, did not appeal. Apparently Soo had come out on top, but that victory came with a high cost. Soo, surprised by the decision, had no real merger plan in place. Further, it had to assume enormous debt to finance the acquisition: $187 million in cash, on top of which it had to assume $383 million of Milwaukee Road debt. The large debt was a bitter pill for Soo to swallow: during the Murray era, cash flow was such that Soo paid for many of its new diesels with cash. In addition, the Milwaukee's right of way, despite many upgrades, was still substandard and suffered from deferred maintenance. The railroad began losing money.

Meanwhile, C&NW began a profitable upsurge, thanks mostly to its tapping into Wyoming's Powder River Basin coal fields in 1984 with help from eventual merger partner Union Pacific. More important, C&NW wasn't saddled with debt from a Milwaukee purchase. Eventually, Cavanaugh lost his job. Parent Canadian Pacific first tried to sell the Soo Line, then changed its mind and acquired full ownership in 1990. As a result, Soo lost its separate identity and became the Heavy Haul Division of CP Rail.

It could be mistaken for a time freight in the 1960s, but the date is March 8, 1987, as a pair of GP30s handle Superior-Chicago train 4 at Marsh siding north of Allenton, Wis. Meeting no. 4 is train 11, bound for Gladstone and Sault Ste. Marie, with freshly repainted caboose 119 guarding the rear. — *Otto P. Dobnick*

2

THOSE LAKE STATES DAYS

THE FAST-CHANGING SOO

Rapid changes for Midwest railroads in the 1980s left the Soo Line a much different railroad. The Soo/Milwaukee System, as the company preferred to be called after being awarded the Milwaukee Road in February 1985, suddenly had two Chicago-Minneapolis main lines that roughly paralleled each other. Soo Line had too much parallel trackage in Wisconsin and faced some tough choices. Operations immediately began undergoing a transformation.

In August 1985 all Chicago-Minneapolis trains were moved to the higher capacity ex-Milwaukee Road line through La Crosse and Milwaukee. The old Soo main between Owen and the Twin Cities became a quiet branch, and the massive steel arch bridge over the St. Croix River at Somerset took on a cemeterylike silence. Trains from Superior, Wausau, and Stevens Point were also rerouted off the old Soo into Milwaukee to access the former Milwaukee Road line to Chicago. At first, Soo

The most modern power assigned to Lake States Transportation Division by parent Soo were two 2300-horsepower SD39s that Soo Line acquired with the purchase of the 45-mile Minneapolis, Northfield, & Southern Railway in 1982. One of the pair, the only road unit to wear the Lake States name, idles at Shops Yard on April 18, 1987. SW1200s 1216 and 1220 also had the Lake States name added to their red-and-white Soo paint scheme.
—*J. David Ingles*

employed its trackage rights over the Wisconsin & Southern once Milwaukee Road Northern Division) from Rugby Junction to Milwaukee. In October 1986 Soo built a connection at Duplainville, north of Waukesha, linking

27

the former Soo main line with the former Milwaukee Road main line. This allowed trains to avoid the tedious ramble down the Wisconsin & Southern through the northern suburbs of Milwaukee.

The result of these reroutings was most telling on the First Subdivision, the former main line from North Fond du Lac to Chicago. In old Soo Line days, this line carded at least seven regular freights in each direction. Now, south of Duplainville, the CTC and welded rail of this strategic segment hosted but a single weekday local!

The expanded Soo, then the tenth largest railroad in the United States, even rerouted Twin Cities-eastern Canada traffic off its original route through Sault Ste. Marie to the ex-Milwaukee Road to Chicago, then on to Detroit by trackage rights on CSX. The traditional routes through Stevens Point and Sault Ste. Marie, which had kept the company firmly in the black for the past 25 years, were no longer crucial. Soo still had an extensive network of secondary and branch lines, especially in Wisconsin and the Upper Peninsula of Michigan. It recognized that they still generated thousands of carloads, particularly from the paper industry, which had many mills along these lines.

Since the old Soo routes through Wisconsin had become light-density feeders, the company felt that operating costs would have to be trimmed to keep them profitable. Also, the cost of acquiring the Milwaukee Road, which included a physical plant suffering from years of deferred maintenance, had contributed to Soo Line experiencing its first deficit since the 1961 merger that created the tightly run, profitable "New Soo." To remedy this situation, the railroad embarked on a unique experiment. It formed what was essentially a "railroad within a railroad."

A NOBLE EXPERIMENT

This internal railroad was christened the Lake States Transportation Division (LSTD) in February 1986. It consisted of almost all of the secondary and branch lines under the Soo/Milwaukee banner east of the Twin Cities, as well as the recently demoted Chicago-Twin Cities main line through Stevens Point — 2,300 miles of railroad in all. The Lake States system stretched from Chicago to St. Paul and Superior via Waukesha, Fond du Lac, and Stevens Point. It included the original Soo from the Twin Cities to Sault Ste. Marie, and former Milwaukee Road lines from New Lisbon to Tomahawk in the Wisconsin River Valley and from Milwaukee to Green Bay. It also included what was left of the Duluth, South Shore & Atlantic in Upper Michigan, and numerous branches to such places as Ashland, Danbury, and Manitowoc. The Lake States moniker was derived from the geography of the region, bordered by two Great Lakes — Michigan and Superior — and dotted with hundreds of smaller lakes.

Lake States was intended to function as a separate entity. The idea was to operate the system using many of the same principles and techniques successfully employed by other new short lines and regional railroads. Soo hoped that by operating with the mentality and flexibility of a short line, better communication with customers and a quicker response to their needs would result. Lake States could build traffic, explore new marketing strategies, and significantly reduce operating expenses, especially labor costs, through more flexible and productive work-rules. Clearly, the success of this new venture depended not only on a good business climate in Wisconsin, but also on cooperation from labor.

Although still owned by Soo Line, the new regional was provided with its own management structure and began developing an independent marketing program. Headquartered in Stevens Point, its identity ultimately extended all the way down to details such as stationery, promotional items, and an employees timetable. Division officials boldly spoke of this concept as an alternative to the abandonment of light-density lines. They also suggested that in any case, the unprofitable lines in the Upper Peninsula of Michigan would probably have to be spun off.

NEW, BUT OLD

Although Lake States was uncoupled from the main part of the Soo Line in February 1986, its train operations and motive-power assignments remained part of the overall Soo Line system until March 1987. It was originally anticipated that Lake States would be changed from a Soo Line division to a separate subsidiary of the corporation. However, as early as November 1986, Soo had received unsolicited proposals from outside parties who desired to acquire all or part of Lake States. Soo officials indicated that such proposals were being given "serious consideration to determine if a sale would fit our long-term corporate strategy." At the same time, they were asking labor unions for more flexible contracts, including reductions in crew size from four to two persons and new wage provisions. Soo officials made it clear that such changes were crucial to the success of Lake States — otherwise the lines would be abandoned or sold.

On March 1, 1987, train operations and motive power assignments were separated from the Soo, but as a division, not a subsidiary. As a railroad of moderate speed and lighter trains, Lake States provided Soo with a repository for 73 of its oldest locomotives. The fledgling regional was assigned 37 GP9s, all of Soo's 19 remaining GP30s, six GP35s, four Soo and five ex-Milwaukee SW1200s, and two ex-Minneapolis, Northfield & Southern SD39s. Many of these units were resurrected from storage lines at Shoreham Shops in Minneapolis. The youngest were 19 years old, the oldest 33. Other Soo power frequently assisted Lake States trains, including ex-Milwaukee Road GP20s and SD10s, plus GP40s and SD40-2s of both Soo and Milwaukee heritage. Twelve leased Conrail GP38s augmented the Lake States fleet. While these units could operate in any combination, solid consists of GP9s, GP30s, and GP35s were not uncommon. From trackside, it appeared as if the 1960s had somehow reappeared, but with a little more rust.

Operations were modified to represent the traffic flows of Lake States as a separate railroad. The most obvious sign was the change from mainline through trains to trains intended to handle originating and terminating traffic between central Wisconsin and Chicago. Lake States carded 28 regular freights, largely on a five- or six-day-a-week schedule. Most lines except the Chicago-Owen main line saw one pair of trains a day. Freights were redesignated with one- and two-digit numbers reminiscent of Soo Line freight and passenger trains on the same routes during the 1950s and 1960s. For example, Lake States 3 and 4 operated between Chicago and Superior along much the same route as Soo Line passenger trains 3 and 4, the *Laker*. Lake States 9 and 10 operated between St. Paul and Argonne along the same route as Soo passenger trains 9 and 10, the *Atlantic Limited*. Only the overnight "Sprint" intermodal trains between Green Bay and Chicago rated three-digit numbers similar to those that

On March 1, 1987, the Lake States Transportation Division began operating trains as a separate railroad, utilizing a fleet of Soo's oldest locomotives. The first Lake States train 17, en route from Belt Railway of Chicago's Clearing Yard to Stevens Point, grinds out of the siding at Rugby Junction, Wis. Soo's first GP30, 700, leads GP35 730 and GP30 705. Keeping the fleet of old locomotives operating proved to be a challenge for Lake States.
— *Otto P. Dobnick*

On an exceptionally warm April 17, 1987, afternoon, train 18 from Ashland is heading for Park Falls and Stevens Point with pulpwood logs and wood chips. The train has completed its work at Mellen, and will follow the banks of the Bad River for the next 16 miles through the Penokee Range, a stretch of rugged hills that halted construction of the original Wisconsin Central for four years. — *Otto P. Dobnick*

Powered by four GP9s, train 19 roars through Van Dyne on its way from Shops Yard to Green Bay on the afternoon of August 23, 1987. The first and last units, 2550 and 4231 (nee 556), were delivered in 1954 and 1955, respectively, and were equipped for passenger service. Until 1965, both units often powered the *Laker* over this same track. — *Otto P. Dobnick*

Soo had used prior to the formation of Lake States. LSTD freely utilized the new Duplainville connecting track, operating all three of its westbound freights and two of its three eastbound Shops Yard-Chicago freights via Milwaukee. Except for a Waukesha-Schiller Park local, only a lone eastbound train ventured south of Duplainville on the old Soo. During mid-1987, even this time freight was moved over to the former Milwaukee Road line.

No major terminal yards were specifically included as part of Lake States. In Chicago, Lake States trains used Soo Line's Bensenville Yard, inherited from the Milwaukee Road, or Belt Railway of Chicago's Clearing Yard. Only the local freight out of Waukesha continued to use Schiller Park. In Superior, Lake States used Soo's Stinson Avenue Yard. Lake States' Twin Cities train from Stevens Point made it only as far as suburban Withrow, Minnesota (just east of the Twin Cities), where it handed over its cars for St. Paul to the Lake States train from Argonne and Ladysmith. Stevens Point and Shops Yard at North Fond du Lac became the principal online classification yards. Operationally, Lake States was a definite precursor of Wisconsin Central.

Lake States trains remained separate from those of Soo up to the sale to Wisconsin Central. However, during late summer and early fall 1987, the separation of Lake States and Soo power seemed to become less strict, as black-and-orange ex-Milwaukee Road locomotives started to appear regularly on many Lake States trains. As the sale of Lake States became more certain, the new unit's autonomy began to disappear as various management functions and positions were folded back into the Soo Line organization.

DECISION TIME

It did not take Soo Line management very long to make up its mind about its regional offspring. While some Lake States lines were unprofitable, others did make money even though the division as a whole was regarded as light-density. Soo Line decision-makers claimed that traffic levels continued to be soft, competition from trucking was stiff, and the necessary work-rule changes were not forthcoming. Reportedly, some — or maybe even most — labor unions recognized the need for change, and were willing to agree to work-rule changes, but at least one major union did not. Soo concluded that burdened with the combination of light traffic, traditional work rules, and Class 1 expenses, Lake States could not cover its costs.

And Soo Line needed cash. Selling Lake States could raise funds to help reduce the large debt incurred when Soo Line was awarded the Milwaukee Road. Soo Line announced that Lake States Transportation Division was for sale, preferably as a complete and potentially viable system. Soo line reached the same conclusion that other Class 1s of the time, such as CP Rail and Burlington Northern, did: the in-house regional subsidiary didn't work. After negotiating with several parties interested in purchasing all or part of Lake States, Soo announced on April 3, 1987, that the unit would be sold to a new firm, Wisconsin Central Ltd. There would be no further chance for testing the regional "railroad-within-a-railroad" theory under the Lake States name. In an era of new regional railroads, Lake States reinforced the idea that a start-up regional would require a brand new company and not be a division of an established carrier.

The first Wisconsin Central train to depart Shops Yard was T046, the Milwaukee turn. GP30s 703 and 707 and GP35 723 — with fresh white paint covering the large Soo lettering — left North Fond du Lac at 1:15 p.m. with 6,726 tons. Less than 45 minutes later, the new Wisconsin Central was cresting Byron Hill for the first time. — *Kenneth Craig*

3

BAPTISM BY FIRE

ON YOUR MARK, GET SET . . .

When Soo's "For Sale" sign went up on Lake States, it caught the eye of several potential buyers, among them a group of railroad officials who had years of experience with Chicago & North Western and Milwaukee Road. Heading this group were two men, Edward A. Burkhardt, who would become WC's first President and Chief Executive Officer, and Thomas F. Power Jr., who would be Executive Vice President and Chief Financial Officer. Burkhardt had spent the last 20 of his 27 railroad career years with C&NW, much of them in operations and most recently as Vice President–Transportation. Power had spent the last 17 of his 21 railroad years with Milwaukee Road, serving most recently as Vice President–Reorganization and Chief Financial Officer during the railroad's reorganization. Other backers included former Illinois governor and former Milwaukee Road trustee Richard B. Ogilvie.

Both Burkhardt and Power had watched as rail traffic in the Midwest was diverted to trucks and opportunities

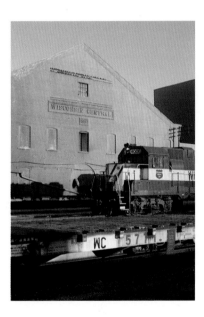

The Wisconsin Central shop in Waukesha opened in 1887 and was closed in 1900. It was leased for use as a foundry, but when it closed in the late 1980s the property reverted to the railroad, by then the new WC. On March 18, 1988, GP35m 4008, assigned to local switching, stands guard over this bit of namesake heritage. Unfortunately the old wall bearing the name collapsed before action to preserve it could be taken. — *J. David Ingles*

for new rail traffic passed by. It was their contention that this occurred because railroads were encumbered by labor rules and restrictions, traditional operating methods, and — according to some — a certain lack of initiative for

35

attracting business. Railroads had become inflexible and unable to react quickly with cost-competitive services. In spite of deregulation and the inherent efficiencies of rail, rates and services offered by truckers continued to undercut what railroads offered.

At the same time, spun-off portions of Class 1 systems seemed to provide an opportunity for a fresh approach and a more productive way of doing things. Burkhardt, Power, and others considered several lines as possible regionals, among them the Chicago & North Western lines north of Green Bay. Ultimately, the Lake States property appeared to be the most attractive. On April 3, 1987, after considering other offers, Soo Line chose Burkhardt and Power's group and announced it had reached a sale agreement. The new owner would be a new company with an almost forgotten name: Wisconsin Central.

Picking the name and a logo was probably the principals' easiest task in starting the company. The name was an easy choice, harking back to the turn-of-the-century railroad of the same name that had constructed many of the same routes. The shield used by the old WC made a distinctive emblem. It had virtually disappeared upon the lease of the original WC by the Soo in 1909, although railroaders and historians with sharp eyes could spot the occasional yellow shield-shaped switchstand targets along old WC lines. Until 1994, a giant shield remained inlaid on a wall of the original WC freight house in downtown Minneapolis.

Wisconsin Central's founders started putting together a railroad. Operations and customer service would be centered at Stevens Point, while corporate headquarters would be near Chicago, in suburban Rosemont. The railroad's original corporate structure was relatively simple. It was operated by Wisconsin Central Ltd. (WCL), which is still the largest and most prominent subsidiary of a holding company known as Wisconsin Central Transportation Corporation. Formed in April 1987 by five men including Burkhardt and Power, the firm was originally privately held. Stock was owned by the lending institutions that provided capital for purchase and start-up, and by senior management, company founders, and a small number of outside investors. Another subsidiary, WCL Railcars, Inc., owned locomotives and cars and leased them to the railroad. WC leased locomotives and cars from other sources, too, such as General Electric Leasing, Brae, and the Oxford Group. WCL Railcars remains separate because of the way in which financing for the equipment was set up. Another subsidiary, Wisconsin Bridges Inc., was created to hold the stock of Sault Ste. Marie Bridge Co., a company owned at the time of purchase equally by Soo Line and Canadian Pacific.

Financing was assembled through the small leveraged buyout market. The founders, together with Berkshire Partners, a company that arranges funds and invests in new companies, provided $15 million in equity toward the project. A syndicate of seven banks provided about $100 million in long-term loans and $10 million in revolving credit for use as working capital. In addition, $20 million in subordinated debt was borrowed from New York Life. Start-up investment totaled about $145 million. $122 million went to Soo Line to buy Lake States, $13 million was used as working capital, and $10 million went for start-up, locomotive, rolling stock, and financing expenses.

In July 1987 the new WC advised Soo Line that it had agreed to terms with its financing sources. Senior management was in place and the hiring of employees was under way. Negotiations had begun for the acquisition of locomotives and freight cars. By September, WC had reached direct delivery agreements with seven connecting carriers at Chicago.

For WC, the most important emphasis was on attracting qualified employees. Priority was given to Lake States people because their experience and knowledge would obviously be valuable. During summer 1987, about 400 Soo employees working on Lakes States accepted jobs with WC. Most of these were maintenance-of-way, shop, and mechanical forces. Only a handful of operating people, particularly dispatchers, elected to stay with WC; most wanting to retain their seniority with Soo. Thus, most WC train service and clerical personnel were new hires. At start-up, employees and their families relocated from 42 states. In one instance, five railroaders from the same Indiana family hired on, swelling the population of Stevens Point by 22. Management and marketing people were mostly from C&NW and Milwaukee Road, but also from Soo and Lake States.

DO NOT PASS GO . . . YET

Finally, a date was set: September 11, 1987. Management expected to assume operations of Lake States under Interstate Commerce Commission (ICC) exemption procedures. Accordingly, a petition was submitted to the ICC on September 4 to begin operations on September 11. Employees, locomotives, equipment, and data management systems were ready to go. Ed Burkhardt noted, "A very fine-tuned, exacting plan was in place based on a September 11 start-up." When the 11th rolled around, however, the intended start-up became the start of WC's baptism by fire.

On the very day WC was to take over, the ICC — prodded by labor unions and a few elected public officials — made a surprising and unprecedented decision and stayed the transaction. Wisconsin Central management, employees, and shippers were astonished. The ICC issued a 45-day delay through October 26 so it could study the sale further. The Commission made it clear that it was not challenging the legality of the sale, but wanted to consider the "unique issues" involved in this "unusually large and significant" transaction. Meanwhile, new employees had to be held away and locomotives leased to other parties on a short-term basis. Computer systems collected dust, not data. During this time, 400 employees who resigned from Soo to start with WC had to be reinstated. Those not coming from the Soo had quit other jobs but now had to wait.

An outpouring of letters, telegrams, and phone calls from shippers, public officials, community leaders, and employees changed the ICC's mind. As suddenly as it stopped the transaction on September 11, the ICC announced on October 8 that it was lifting the stay at 12:01 a.m., Sunday, October 11. With three days notice, the closing process was triggered. Burkhardt said, "We'll be running as of Sunday morning." The actual closing process took all day Saturday and into Sunday morning, but by 4 a.m., officials had churned through mountains of paperwork, signed documents, and handled last-minute negotiations. After an estimated 80,000 pages of closing documents, the Soo was $122 million richer. Burkhardt summarized the celebration: "I think somebody at the closing had a bottle of champagne and I think I may have had a mouthful, then we went to work."

The transition began immediately. As the last papers were signed, workers at Stevens Point and North Fond du

During WC's first few months, there was little maroon and gold equipment to be found, and many of the green ex-Burlington Northern SD45's had yet to arrive. In October 1987, T006 accelerates across I-35W in suburban New Brighton, Minn., utilizing WC's trackage rights over Soo Line. The train is destined for Stevens Point with horsepower provided by leased Soo GP20 963, GP9 2405, and WC GP35 723. — *Fred Hyde*

At 7:23 a.m., Sunday, October 11, 1987, in Stevens Point, Wis., engineer Brian Miller opened the throttle on former Soo GP35 726, and the first Wisconsin Central train (T002) was rolling. Conductor on this sunny Sunday morning was R. Wilke. Train T002 departed Point with leased Soo GP9 2412 and former Soo GP30 710 in addition to GP35 726, pulling 45 loads and 43 empties totaling 5,465 tons. By midmorning the train was trundling down Division Street in Oshkosh. It arrived at Shops Yard in North Fond du Lac at 11:25 a.m.
— *Charles Heraver*

Lac began restenciling equipment with WC reporting marks. WC initials were stenciled onto the cab of some ex-Soo locomotives and the "SOO" on the sides was covered with matching white paint. At the same time, track and bridges were inspected, and waybill and car record information was checked and updated. At 7:23 a.m. on that quiet Sunday morning, the first Wisconsin Central freight train departed Stevens Point for North Fond du Lac. The new WC was a real, live, operating railroad.

OUT OF THE FRYING PAN . . .

However, the reincarnated WC would not come on line without growing pains. While WC had been ready for September 11, it wasn't ready for October 11. Referring to the four weeks in limbo, Burkhardt said, "Our planning totally collapsed during that period," noting it was not certain when or even if the ICC stay would be lifted. Whenever the start-up was to occur, a monumental job lay ahead because of the wholesale change of employees. Nevertheless, the company could not let the October 11 opportunity slip by.

Several complications set in right away. First, when the postponement occurred, the lessor providing 40 SD45 locomotives that were to be the backbone of the fleet sent 20 units to Southern Pacific for the remainder of the year. Then new employees, who would be unfamiliar with the railroad's operating practices, customer requirements, and managing the critical waybill information, wound up elsewhere, at least temporarily. But the big surprise was that the waybill information for 2,700 cars on the railroad at the time of the sale was useless. It was suspected that an apparently disgruntled person leaving with the Soo had scrambled the information as a parting shot.

Thus the new railroad started business on virtually overnight notice, with insufficient motive power to move 2,700 mystery cars, using a skeleton staff unfamiliar with the territory. The result was predictable. For the first two months, train schedules were almost nonexistent, and train crew workdays were likely to end almost anywhere. On the main line between Chicago and Fond du Lac, for example, taxicabs from as far away as Neenah were common visitors to Waukesha, ferrying crews to rescue stranded trains. Customers understandably were concerned about the delivery of vital raw materials and supplies, and requests for delivery of "hot" carloads were not uncommon.

Immediately, the fledgling railroad started to fight back, reassembling the work force, locomotive fleet, and schedules that had been ready to go in September. To alleviate the power shortage, WC retained some of Soo's Lake States GP9s for several weeks and leased 22 other units until the stray SD45's were available in December.

Every usable track seemed to be filled with freight cars, either "lost" ones being identified and sorted out, or cars intentionally switched there. To expedite traffic through Fond du Lac while operating people were learning the territory, the classification of southbound traffic was relocated to a series of passing sidings along the main line from North Fond du Lac to Burlington. Pre-blocked cuts of cars would be set out for pick-up by following trains. This "block-swapping" began in early November and allowed Shops Yard to be devoted to northbound classification work. After yard capacity was added in mid-December, block-swapping was stopped and all yard work returned to Shops.

To get record-keeping and waybill work under control during the first five weeks, additional employees were recruited, temporary help hired, and corporate headquarters staff sent to the field, helping to move trains and identify cars. The antidote for the spoiled waybill records turned out to be inspection of every car on the property.

As 1987 ended, things were looking much brighter, with most of the equipment and personnel in place. Train schedules became more reliable, and service levels dramatically improved. The backlog of cars had been cleaned up, and shipper complaints were turning into compliments. On the first payday, October 28, the company issued 531 checks; by November 11, there were 713.

To anyone watching WC's start-up ordeal, such a dramatic turnaround within a few months was astonishing. Top management proudly speaks of the dedication, attitude, and perseverance of the employees during this turbulent period. Explains Burkhardt with pride, "The difficulty of getting started under these kinds of conditions served to very much solidify the work force from top to the bottom. The problems served as a catalyst to get everybody working together. We had a lot of things that have really turned out to be great in terms of our relationship with the people who wound up working on this property." The ordeal of late 1987 was over none too soon: it was estimated the four-week delay cost WC up to $8 million.

A RAILROAD BY ANY OTHER NAME

For $122 million, WC purchased a lot of railroad from Soo Line in terms of fixed plant and property. The new Wisconsin Central was aptly named. The system, 2,047 route-miles at start-up, was made up of medium- to light-density lines that stretched like a net across central and northern Wisconsin. The traffic base rested largely on paper, pulp, and converting mills. Much of the inbound materials to these mills and the outbound products was directed onto the WC main between Stevens Point and Chicago, making the system function like a funnel aimed at Chicago connections. WC had to use trackage rights over Soo Line to reach the major gateways of Minneapolis, St. Paul, Duluth, and Superior. However, at Chicago (as at Sault Ste. Marie) WC owned its own railroad.

The centerpiece of the railroad remained 421 miles of Soo's former main line between Forest Park, Ill. — where trains enter Baltimore & Ohio Chicago Terminal trackage in Chicago — and Withrow, Minn., where they use trackage retained by Soo into the Twin Cities. Most of the line was in excellent physical condition and boasted welded rail. Soo freights operated at 40 mph over this main line, but within a year after start up, WC raised speeds to 50 mph south of Neenah (later extended to Stevens Point). Centralized traffic control (CTC) was in operation over 285 miles of line between Schiller Park and Owen. WC disconnected the 42-mile stretch of CTC between Owen and Chippewa Falls during the winter of 1987–1988 because of the small number of trains.

Another crucial line for the WC was the Valley Subdivision linking New Lisbon, Junction City, and Tomahawk. This former Milwaukee Road line penetrates the heart of central Wisconsin papermaking territory and serves many of WC's largest customers. It was rebuilt by the Milwaukee in 1981 and 1982 in part with federal 4R Act funds, and it has welded rail. WC officials knew what they were buying and gave Soo Line credit for emphasizing proper track maintenance on its main lines.

The sale agreement was straightforward. It included the railroad property and all associated buildings, structures, tracks, signals, and even adjoining property not

In WC's first few years, maroon locomotives were still quite rare. Other than the required restenciling of reporting marks to show ownership, widespread repainting would have to wait until more important car, yard, track, and other roadway improvements were made. At the Gladstone, Mich., roundhouse on a cold February evening, GP30 716 and SD45 6417 await assignments. — *Steve Glischinski*

In May 1989 the North Fond du Lac shop complex had changed little from Soo Line days. In the middle are the turntable and roundhouse. Just beyond is the diesel shop, erected in 1955, and flanking both sides of the transfer table are the car repair shop and stores buildings. Over the next few years, WC would begin major improvements, including remodeling the roundhouse and modernization of the fuel rack and servicing area. To the east of the complex can be seen the Fox River Valley Railroad main line and yard, which would become WC's west-bound classification yard after the FRVR was acquired in 1993.
— *Zephyr Graphics/Andover Junction Publications*

Since day one, the shops at North Fond du Lac have been kept busy. Much of the early work concentrated on repairing cars purchased from other railroads. Freshly repainted, a rehabilitated boxcar receives some underframe repairs before re-entering service. Employees at "North Fondy" are proud of their work and have held several open houses for the public.
— *Pete Briggs*

used for rail operations. It also included trackage rights for both WC and Soo, and certain maintenance tools, equipment, and supplies, but did not include locomotives or freight cars, which were acquired separately. Bad order cars and other scrap were excluded unless these items remained on the property after 90 days.

The agreement forbade WC trains from handling bridge traffic on the segments Soo retained from Ladysmith to Superior and from Withrow to the Twin Cities. Although Soo retained ownership of the Ladysmith-Superior segment, it had no operation on this line after the sale except for a few detours; WC maintained it and handled all local traffic. There were no restrictions on WC at Chicago or Sault Ste. Marie. With four gateways, including unrestricted access to Chicago, WC had ensured that it would not be captive to Soo Line or any other railroad.

The restriction on overhead moves was intended to keep WC from competing for traffic from western Canada routed over Duluth, Winnipeg & Pacific to Superior and then to other carriers. Much of this is lumber traffic, but because profit margins on overhead traffic can be very slim, the inability to compete for it did not bother WC officials at the time. Burkhardt explained, "[handling bridge traffic] would have added more to the purchase price than the near-term benefit. For now, we want to concentrate on serving shippers in the region." Later, WC would decide the traffic was valuable.

Because the topography in Wisconsin and Michigan's Upper Peninsula is anything but flat — testimony to the carving effects of glaciers — WC inherited a lot of wood and steel trestles and bridges. By far the largest is the half-mile-long, five-arch bridge spanning the St. Croix River on the Wisconsin-Minnesota border. Massive structures also span the Wisconsin River and other northwoods waterways. Between the two Sault Ste. Maries, the railroad crosses the St. Mary's River (and the international border) on drawbridges of three different types.

The sale included the shops at North Fond du Lac and Stevens Point, 18 classification yards, 11 roundhouses and turntables, a variety of depots, freight houses and other buildings, and two monstrous, long-unused concrete-and-steel iron ore docks in Ashland and Marquette. Excluded from the sale were machinery, tools, and supplies used at the North Fond du Lac shop, if removed by Soo within nine months. Soo reserved the right to use the shop during that time. Some stone, brick, and cinderblock depots of original-WC heritage survived to the new WC in places such as Waukesha, Waupaca, Marshfield, New Richmond, and Osceola. To its credit, the new WC continued Soo's frugal ways and didn't dispose of any property prematurely.

PAPER IS THE NAME OF THE GAME

A railroad is more than track and structures — it's also freight traffic. Wisconsin may be known as America's Dairyland, but much of its economic muscle is provided by the paper industry, which served as the primary traffic base for the new WC. Wisconsin has been the nation's leading papermaking state since 1953, and its mills consistently produce about 12 percent of the nation's output, almost twice the volume of the next closest state, Maine. Although the industry's fortunes — and profits — can be cyclical, production volumes are normally stable unless there is a dramatic change in economic conditions. This means a steady base of traffic for WC: in 1987 and 1988,

44

the paper industry accounted for 60 percent of all WC carloads. Both writing and printing papers, as well as tissue and household papers are considered necessities, and many producers in WC's territory continue to expand.

Of the 52 active pulp and paper mill facilities throughout the Badger State in 1987, WC served 24 when it began operations. In addition, two more mills were on the Marinette, Tomahawk & Western (now Tomahawk Railway), and another was on an isolated branch of the Lake Superior & Ishpeming (LS&I). Both lines interchanged only with WC. Four of the seven mills in Michigan's Upper Peninsula, plus one in Sault Ste. Marie, Ontario, and eight major paper-converting mills in Wisconsin were also by served WC. Many of the paper industry's big names were represented on WC sidings: Consolidated Papers, Flambeau Paper, Georgia-Pacific, James River, Kimberly-Clark, Mead, Mosinee Paper, Procter & Gamble, and Weyerhaeuser. Most of the mills are concentrated in the Fox River valley between Neenah and Green Bay, and the Wisconsin River valley between Nekoosa and Tomahawk. In the fiercely competitive paper industry, minimizing inventory and maintaining round-the-clock production demands consistent responsive transportation. As a result, many of WC's operations are geared toward the mill sites. Said Ed Burkhardt, "The paper mills run seven days a week and so should we."

At the end of 1988, WC's first full year in operation, the top 15 shippers (in revenues) represented 51 percent of all traffic; 11 of these were paper and pulp mills. Two more customers were paper-related: Eddy Forest Products, a supplier of wood pulp, and Quad/Graphics, a large printing firm with plants on WC at Duplainville, Sussex, and Lomira that received daily shipments of paper for printing magazines and consumer catalogs. "Quad" was the railroad's largest receiver of printing paper. The remaining two of the top 15 were Wisconsin Public Service, which received coal at its Green Bay and Weston (Wausau) power plants; and GAF, a producer of roofing pellets at Kremlin in northeastern Wisconsin.

At start-up the 40 percent of WC's traffic that was not paper related encompassed a wide variety of commodities. Some examples: at Burlington, Foster Forbes received high-quality sand for glass bottle manufacturing and Nestle Foods received ingredients for chocolate products. At Waukesha, Cooper Electric loaded large electric transformers, many of which were oversize. At Fond du Lac, Larson Canning and Sadoff Scrap sent out boxcars and gondolas with loads. On the west end, trainloads of trap rock for ballast on WC and other railroads came from Dresser. In the Upper Peninsula, seasonal gondola shipments of copper concentrate were delivered to White Pine Mine. At Schofield, just outside Wausau, the J. I. Case plant rolled new tractors onto flatcars, and at Sault Ste. Marie, Ont., Algoma Steel loaded outbound cars with steel products. At the end of 1988, WC's traffic mix by revenue carloads broke down like this: pulp, fibers, and lumber, 24 percent; paper, 14; pulpboard, 12; clay and minerals, 11; coal, 9; chemicals, 9; intermodal, 7; food and grain, 7; steel and scrap, 6; and other, 1.

PEOPLE RUN THE TRAINS

To move this traffic, WC patterned its train operations after Lake States'. It set up a hub-and-spoke system, with Stevens Point and Shops Yard as the two major hubs. Neenah and Gladstone were minor hubs. There were three types of trains: through freights, local freights, and

Wisconsin Central's original fleet of switchers comprised units from Houston Belt & Terminal, Missouri Pacific, Southern Pacific, and Cotton Belt. On March 6, 1988, two unrepainted SW1200s —ex-Cotton Belt 2260 and ex-MP 1107 — sort the yard tracks at Shops Yard. In only a few months, they will appear in maroon and gold as WC 1235 and 1230. — *Otto P. Dobnick*

During the start-up ordeal, one of the most crucial jobs was that of train dispatcher. Since most train crews were new to the territory, the Stevens Point dispatchers spent three hectic and sometimes frustrating months informing crews where sidings were, on which yard tracks cars were to be found, where customers wanted cars spotted, even telling road trains what the next station would be. The collective knowledge of the dispatching crew, most of whom came from the Soo Line, was indispensable during WC's early days. — *Otto P. Dobnick*

The Customer Service Center (CSC) in the former Soo passenger depot at Stevens Point is a centralized service bureau staffed seven days a week. Customers can order equipment, trace cars, and obtain answers to service inquiries. The center handles all the railroad's origin billing and agency functions. CSC people frequently talk with dispatchers to expedite car movements, as Diane Jones is doing here. Casey Jones, the WC-bedecked bear, part of WC employees' involvement with the Operation Lifesaver program, takes a rest from helping Diane teach youngsters safety around railroad tracks. — *Otto P. Dobnick*

yard switchers, designated on paperwork and in computer files by T-, L-, and Y-numbers, respectively. For example, through freights were designated by the letter T, then a three-digit number, such as T005. Locals and road switchers carried an L designation, such as L044, while yard jobs carried a Y prefix. Like the basic service patterns, the train numbers were a refinement and expansion of Lake States designations. In 1993, when WC subsidiary Fox Valley & Western (FV&W) acquired the Green Bay & Western and Fox River Valley railroads, locals and yard jobs on FV&W lines were given an F prefix, such as FL076 or FY092.

A major key to Wisconsin Central's use of resources was that its work force could be versatile and did not have to contend with an encyclopedia of restrictive work rules. Train crews could be far more flexible than on traditional railroads. For example, a crew in Chicago might have first taken a transfer run, then relieved an inbound road crew, both during the same shift. In North Fond du Lac, a switch crew could work the yard, then go into Fond du Lac proper with a switcher to pick up a car, return to the yard, then hop on a pair of SD45s to push an ore train up Byron Hill. Most train crews had two persons, but switch crews that sorted the major yards and on occasion a few local freights — such as the Stevens Point-Medford turn — warranted three because of the large amount of ground work.

During its first two years, the average crew size on WC was 2.2 persons, compared with 4.8 on Lake States. Said Burkhardt at the time, "The difference is entirely in the number of people that we use to accomplish a task." This means that the labor ratio (percentage of revenue that is labor expense) for WC was 30 percent, compared with an industrywide average of 45 percent, and 50 percent on some Midwestern Class 1s. This was important to

a light-density system such as WC, where annual revenue per mile in 1988 was only $50,000, vs. $201,000 for Class 1s. Without 108-mile work days for train crews and arbitraries dictating what work they can perform, "Wisconsin Central runs a lot more trains and a much more fluid operation than Soo Line could afford (on the same lines)," Burkhardt said in 1990.

This flexibility led to cross-training of employees. If more people were needed in a specific area, or if someone wanted to do a different job, that opportunity was available. Burkhardt and Power aimed for stability in the work force, minimizing the layoffs and call-backs that are demoralizing to employees. Burkhardt said in 1990, "Having the ability to move people around helps a great deal. We want to have a high degree of mobility of our work force. People can bid for any job in the whole company for which they're qualified . . . or we'll help them get qualified." For example, many engineers and conductors could perform either job, allowing for flexibility in train crew assignments. Some maintenance-of-way employees have worked in the shops during the winter, and others have gone into train service.

One man who had been with the Soo for 10 years as a section foreman started on WC in the same capacity. He was trained to use the Transportation System Control computer in operations, became an industrial representative who did load measuring and inspection of high-wide loads, and was qualified as a train conductor.

In this flexible environment, employees were ready to help each other more than they might otherwise. Conductors often helped each other's trains get through congested areas, and trainmasters often assisted train crews with moving cars and trains.

Green SD45s were common from 1987 through 1993, since high demand for the units kept them on the road as much as possible. On March 6, 1988, "green gators" — as some crews referred to them — 6660 and 6510, led by GP35m 4006, glide through the frozen marshlands near Theresa, Wisconsin. The units are in charge of train T002 out of Shops Yard, destined for Illinois Central's Markham Yard south of Chicago. In August 1990, the train was redesignated as T040 south of Shops. — *Otto P. Dobnick*

In a message to employees at the end of WC's first year, President Ed Burkhardt noted, "This has been a very commendable year in many respects. The high level of customer satisfaction that WC enjoys is directly attributable to the great personal interest that each of you has demonstrated in the company since start-up." Wisconsin Central commemorated its first year by decorating SD45 6655 in a special paint scheme which soon became the railroad's standard. Ironically, 6655 would be the first SD45 retired, even as WC amassed over 100 other SD45s. — *Otto P. Dobnick*

How did this look from an employee's perspective? So far, there have been no unions on Wisconsin Central, although employees have the legal right to elect a collective-bargaining representative if they so chose. All employees are salaried, based on the average time required for a specific job. Because of the regional nature of WC, salaries at start-up were somewhat below the rail industry average, but averaged well above the annual wage earned by Wisconsin workers overall. WC offered a full range of benefits, including a 401(k) retirement-investment plan and a profit-sharing program. In spite of the shaky start-up, employees received a $100 Christmas bonus at the end of 1987 and $200 at the end of 1988. Since 1988, there have been annual salary raises and profit-sharing payouts.

Several times a year, Burkhardt and other top officials meet at various locations with employees, who are encouraged to ask questions. Any employee can talk directly with Burkhardt or any other official or manager. Said Power in 1990, "We want to create a family relationship with our employees, make them a part of the company, not just hired hands." He added, "Customers and employees are the only things that make companies go."

Following start-up, it was easy to find a high level of dedication and enthusiasm among WC people. Get them talking and you'd hear that it was nice to be working for a railroad that was expanding and reinvesting in the plant and equipment, and whose managers listened to your suggestions. Employees were proud of getting the railroad going and enthusiastic about how fast cars moved through the system. Many WC train crews talked of the frustration in watching their former railroad employers let traffic disappear, reduce service, and abandon lines. Even though many of jobs on WC had the same hardships as those on

any other railroad — a lot of third-shift hours, a potentially dangerous work environment, and the necessity of being away from home at odd hours — Wisconsin Central, they said, was doing things right. While some of this enthusiasm faded with the transition from start-up to routine operations, most WC employees still agree that working for the nation's largest regional is still preferable to working for a Class 1.

DON'T LOOK BACK

Immediately after sorting out the start-up chaos, the railroad started earning its well-regarded reputation. It improved the quality of the fixed plant and equipment, improved service to customers, and aggressively sought new traffic. This aggressive posture and the results it would generate over the next nine years quickly earned it an unusually positive reputation with shippers and the region in general.

WC embarked on an ambitious program of fine-tuning its lines. Some changes and improvements didn't even wait until the start-up confusion subsided. During its first months, work was concentrated on eliminating slow orders, resurfacing lines such as the Ashland Sub, adding capacity at Shops Yard, and improving the Minnesota Commercial interchange at New Brighton, Minn. The 15-mile Menasha-Hilbert section of the Manitowoc Sub, dormant for two years, was reopened on November 2, 1987, when a 65-car train departed Neenah for Manitowoc. By the end of 1988, WC had applied 133,000 tons of crushed rock (most from quarries at Dresser, Wis.), tamped and aligned 400 miles of track, and replaced nearly 70,000 ties. By comparison, Lake States had installed only 18,000 ties and performed only nominal trackwork in its last year.

By the end of 1988 Wisconsin Central had procured additional trackage rights to effect direct connections with more railroads in Chicago, including Burlington Northern, Chicago Central, Chicago Rail Link, Manufacturers' Junction, and Illinois Central.

Improvements also were made to administrative and office areas. The Customer Service Center in Stevens Point moved from a Main Street office into the remodeled passenger depot. The soon-to-be-familiar red WC shield appeared on stationery, buildings, and bridges. In April 1988, WC general offices relocated from temporary quarters in Park Ridge to the ninth floor of a larger Rosemont office building, with a distant view of the Schiller Park yard.

WC's mechanical department started car-repair programs immediately, and quickly expanded and improved the fleet of freight cars. At start-up the fleet numbered 2,900; by the end of 1988 WC had 4,200 freight cars. About half were boxcars; the rest of the fleet included covered hoppers, gondolas, flatcars, and hopper cars. By contrast, Soo Line had assigned only 2,600 cars to Lake States.

Most of the cars that went through the repair shop were repainted. Boxcars came out maroon with gold lettering, covered hoppers gray with maroon lettering, and open-top hopper and gondolas black with white lettering. However, after crews complained about the lack of visibility of the black cars, they were changed to gray with maroon lettering. Gondolas used for coiled steel were given maroon paint because of their special service. Shield logos were applied to boxcars, but hoppers and gons received billboard lettering. About two-thirds of WC's inherited cars came from Soo Line (including Milwaukee Road and MN&S cars). By mid-1989 about 10 percent of WC's car fleet had been shopped.

In Soo Line days, the busy North Fond du Lac shops could tackle almost any job, and even mass-produced new boxcars on occasion. During its last years as a Soo facility, employment and activity dwindled, but the arrival of WC essentially reopened the shop, which provided employment for more than 100 by the end of 1988. A major early activity for the shop was churning through the backlog of bad-order cars. Those that required up to 400 man-hours of work were repaired, while those beyond that level were sold to scrap dealers. Car work was also done at Stevens Point and Gladstone, and locomotives were maintained at North Fond du Lac and Stevens Point. North Fond du Lac also did much of the work on the railroad's maintenance-of-way equipment. The shop forces were flexible, with many of the same people working on locomotives and cars.

A large part of improving WC's level of service has been increasing the number of trains and emphasizing connections — with other WC trains as well as connecting railroads — to keep cars moving. As initial operations settled into a pattern, WC increased service not only on main lines, but on secondary and branch lines, where service went from triweekly to five or six days a week. Local switch jobs also were rescheduled or increased. In December 1987, time freights T007 and T008 were added between Stevens Point and Shops Yard, and on October 17, 1988, locals L011 and L012 were added between Stevens Point and Tomahawk, primarily for traffic interchange with the Marinette, Tomahawk & Western Railroad (now Tomahawk Railway).

Most WC freight trains were given regular schedules. As Bill Schauer, WC's Vice President–Marketing, said,

Although this view of train No. 1 arriving at the Neenah yard suggests otherwise, WC never used cabooses on its road trains. However, WC acquired five ex-Milwaukee Road bay window cabooses from Lake States for use on switch and local jobs that involve back-up moves and on work trains. Caboose 17 is being deadheaded to Stevens Point from Shops Yard, having been thoughtfully placed where cabooses belong, at the end of the train. Later, WC would inherit cabooses from the Green Bay & Western and Algoma Central.
— *Otto P. Dobnick*

On July 23, 1988, steam appeared on the modern WC for the first time, as St. Louis Steam Train Association's Frisco 4-8-2 1522 deadheaded from Chicago to North Fond du Lac in preparation for two days of public trips. Here the 1926 Baldwin works through Lomira ferrying a short freight consist. The sleek 1522 was reminiscent of the Soo/WC Mountains that pulled passenger and freight trains over the same rails in the 1930s and 1940s.
— *Robert S. McGonigal*

"Whether there are 10 or 110 cars, our trains move on schedule. They run at the same time every day and aren't held until a certain number of cars are collected."

Wisconsin Central's aggressive marketing approach has been crucial to the traffic growth. Although WC acts like a Class 1 carrier in many ways, its customer-oriented marketing and operating philosophy has been more akin to that of short lines or nonrailroad firms. WC's mission was summarized by its pledge, which has appeared in company marketing and promotional materials: "To offer superior transportation consisting of more frequent, dependable train service, at competitive prices, with proper equipment, accomplished by customer-minded employees."

At start-up, WC had a business plan that conservatively relied on originating, terminating, and local traffic, not on overhead traffic from other railroads. Overhead business is susceptible to diversion to other railroads, making it very competitive, and usually generates small profit margins unless sufficient volume can be secured. WC's marketing efforts were aimed at enlarging the share of freight shipped by existing customers, regaining customers who had shifted to trucks, and serving new shippers. After a stable base of originating and terminating traffic had been assured, certain restrictions imposed by the original sale then could be addressed, such as targeting potentially profitable overhead markets such as iron ore and Canadian traffic.

WC's marketing strategy has involved going out and talking with potential shippers, large and small, who have never used the railroad or who stopped using it years ago. Tom Power said: "You build your base with one or two cars from this guy and one or two from that guy. We're out looking for business and knocking on doors. If our tracks go through a community, we want to know what's in every town, who we can serve from a team track or a transload, or pull up to their dock. Too many old sidings out there haven't been used in a long time, and we're breaking the rust off them."

WC soon proved it could even snare traffic from neighboring lines. In October 1988, the siding to Kimberly-Clark's plastic pellet facility in Neenah was disconnected from Chicago & North Western's line and connected to WC. In March 1988, WC took over the switching contract for Consolidated Papers' mill at Wisconsin Rapids, which Green Bay & Western had switched for 50 years.

Wisconsin Central has had no sales department as such. Customer contact has been largely a function of operations. On-line customer contact work is handled by operations managers and train crews, who talk with shipping people on the loading docks and traffic people in the offices. Train crews and other employees in the field have been responsible for many leads on new customers.

The marketing department in Rosemont is organized by industry, and customers need only talk to one person. In many cases, WC representatives have been able to get rate quotations back to customers in hours, not days.

During its first years, WC marketing efforts concentrated chiefly on pulpwood and piggyback. "Pulpwood is probably our biggest success story insofar as directing traffic off the highways," said Schauer in 1990. During the 1970s, railroads surrendered most northern Wisconsin pulpwood traffic to trucks, claiming it was unprofitable since the raw material was worth less than the cost of moving it. As the pulpwood disappeared from the rails, so did the rails themselves. WC began reclaiming this traffic, by 1989 moving 11,000 carloads of pulpwood logs and 2,000 of wood chips. Major pulpwood consignees have been the Consolidated and Nekoosa mills. The wood comes from the Ashland and Superior lines, Michigan's Upper Peninsula, and interchange from the DM&IR and Nicolet Badger Northern (NBN has since shut down). In 1989 Mosinee Paper, a large on-line mill, resumed shipping pulpwood by rail for the first time in 15 years.

Intermodal traffic was also an early success story. Overnight Chicago-Green Bay trains T218 and T219 (inherited from Soo Line) were WC's first foray into the market. By December 1989 WC could report a 60 percent increase in intermodal volume, handling about 1,200 trailers and containers a month compared with 750 at start-up. During the first three or four years, 218 and 219 were frequently filled out with nonintermodal traffic and eventually changed from five- to six-day operation.

A key to WC's early personalized service and fast transit times was the use of the Transportation Control System (TCS), an integrated set of computer programs for operations management and planning purchased from Union Pacific Technologies. The system was developed by Missouri Pacific and adapted by Union Pacific after their 1982 merger. Wisconsin Central was the first outside buyer of the system. TCS creates trip schedules for each carload; provides shipment data by location, commodity, and type of equipment; generates waybills; prepares work orders for employees; and prints out train operating information. TCS also handles data interchange with other railroads, operations management functions, equipment maintenance records, marketing data, and equipment scheduling. The largest WC users of the TCS are its Customer Service Center and its Operations Control Center.

The WC start-up years ended with some housecleaning activities. WC acquired a tremendous amount of real estate no longer used for railroad purposes. A few parcels of land turned out to be valuable and, in 1989, sales of that property netted $3.1 million. Proceeds were used to help reduce WC's debt.

Also, miscellaneous items were gathered from all over the system, and on August 20, 1988, some 670 of these — from old tariffs and stationery to crossing signals, depot benches, and signs — were auctioned off at Stevens Point to collectors and antique dealers.

Wisconsin Central's new attitude, improved rolling stock and facilities, and aggressive marketing began to pay off in increased carloadings and revenues. In 1988 WC handled almost 145,000 revenue carloads, compared with Lake States' traffic base of 138,000. From operating revenues of $94 million WC netted $3 million, and the railroad turned a profit beginning in March 1988. This resulted in a need for more employees.

The original employment plans were for about 700 people, but average employment for 1988 was 850. The new Wisconsin Central quickly established itself as a railroad synonymous with dependable, responsive, and competitive service, able to increase traffic by diverting it from trucks and convincing former shippers to return to rail service.

It's just after sunrise on June 29, 1994, as the intermodal trailers of Chicago-Green Bay train T219 streak through Duplainville, Wis. T219, along with eastbound counterpart T218, have operated continuously under both Soo and WC ownership. Initiated by Soo on September 8, 1986, as part of its "Sprint" service (the name Sprint was given to Milwaukee Road's specialized intermodal trains in 1978) the trains made WC one of the few regionals to haul significant volumes of piggyback trailers and containers. The trains originally ran on the old Superior Division, but when Soo acquired trackage rights over GB&W between Green Bay and Black Creek on January 2, 1987, they began running via Neenah and Duplainville. The trains continued in operation after the WC purchase, retaining the same numbers. WC soon expanded the service with connecting inter-modal services between Stevens Point and Neenah. — *Jeff Hampton*

4

STABILITY AND STRENGTHENING

A "QUALITY CARRIER"

As Wisconsin Central entered its third year, it had made great strides in customer service as well as operations. The turbulent start-up was behind it, and the company could concentrate on fine-tuning customer service and increasing business. The key to growth was an intense focus on customer service. "We've actually made customer service the responsibility of employees at all levels," WC President Ed Burkhardt said in 1991.

The focus on customer satisfaction resulted in unprecedented recognition from shippers. In 1989 WC was named a "Quality Carrier" by *Distribution* magazine in its annual "Quest for Quality" survey of transportation companies in the United States. Given by the magazine after polling of customers, it is the only award in which shippers rate their carrier's performance on quality of service, convenience, price, and customer satisfaction. WC was one of two railroads named that year and went on to win the award each year through 1995.

The shine on SD45 No. 6582, pictured at New Brighton, Minn., on September 5, 1993, typifies Wisconsin Central's maintenance policy. — *Steve Glischinski*

In 1990 three major customers — Consolidated Papers, CF Industries, and 3M — recognized WC for outstanding service. In 1991 Mead Papers in Groos, Mich. — then the largest mill served by WC — signed a 12-year partnership agreement covering the transportation of paper and raw materials.

The news media began to notice WC's success. In 1988 and 1989, WC was the subject of extensive articles in the Milwaukee *Sentinel* and the Chicago *Tribune*. In 1990 the railroad was the subject of a cover story in *Railway Age* and articles in *Intermodal Age* and *Progressive Railroading*, all trade journals. The popular press also told the WC story, with articles in *Trains* and *Railfan & Railroad* magazines. WC has continued to receive extensive coverage, especially as it has expanded and staved off unionization.

Efforts to improve the physical plant continued in the late 1980s. While Soo Line generally conveyed to WC a property in good condition, it had done no heavy maintenance on WC lines since it purchased the Milwaukee Road in 1985. In WC's first three years, engineering forces played "catch up" with routine maintenance, and the company continued to expend more dollars to improve the physical plant. In 1988 WC installed 64,119 ties and surfaced 368 miles of track. The figures for 1989 were 96,000 ties and 440 miles, plus 147,000 tons of ballast dumped. In 1990 the maintenance budget increased to $12.5 million, with 133,000 ties installed (nearly double 1988's work), 450 miles surfaced, and five miles of welded rail installed between Neenah and Appleton.

By 1990 WC could concentrate on special track rehabilitation programs. One of the largest was rebuilding the 44-mile line between Neenah and Manitowoc, a Lake Michigan port that is home to several important shippers. Soo Line had allowed the track to deteriorate so that the speed limit was down to 10 miles per hour. Thanks to a 50 percent grant and 30 percent low-interest loan from the Wisconsin Department of Transportation, WC rebuilt the track to 25 mph standards. The line took on more importance after the 1993 acquisition of Fox River Valley Railroad, which served several customers in Manitowoc.

Track maintenance is vital in Michigan's Upper Peninsula, where swampy ground had long since swallowed any upgrading efforts the lines received from Soo Line. Armed with a $300,000 loan from the Michigan DOT, WC upgraded 19 miles of track in 1990 between Eustis and Faithorn and surfaced track between Gladstone and Sault Ste. Marie.

Another important branchline upgrade had taken place on the Michigan Division the year before. In August 1989 WC purchased Lake Superior & Ishpeming's 5.5-mile branch from a WC connection at Munising Junction to the Lake Superior port of Munising. The line had been isolated from the rest of LS&I after the railroad abandoned its east end in 1979, but was retained to serve Kimberly-Clark's Munising mill. A single diesel, usually LS&I's last active Alco RS-3, was kept there and a three-person crew drove over from Marquette three times a week to switch the mill. WC has rebuilt the branch with financial assistance from Kimberly-Clark.

In the western reach of the Upper Peninsula, the Copper Range Company revitalized a copper mine at White Pine. It is served by a 14-mile branch off the old DSS&A main at Bergland. During 1988 WC hauled pyrite, a copper concentrate used in smelting, from Marquette over the little-used line from Nestoria to Bergland. WC pulled up most of this line in 1989, so when seasonal operations to White Pine resumed in May 1989, and again in April 1991, WC served White Pine from the west via the 78-mile line from Marengo Junction, Wis.

WC has also handled all-rail movements of West Virginia coal to the mine. Previously it had been transloaded from lakeboats at Ontonagon, Mich., and trucked to White Pine. Subsequently, in addition to coal, WC began moving inbound copper concentrate and grinding equipment and outbound copper cathodes. The future appeared bright, but in July 1995 Copper Range's parent, Inmet Mining Corp., announced that it could not economically justify keeping the underground mine in operation and closed it on September 30, 1995. Copper shipments continued out of the facility into 1996, and on May 28, 1996, mine officials announced a mining project that would pump an iron-bearing acidic solution in the mine. If it is successful, Copper Range could continue to mine copper using this low-cost technique for an additional 15 years, insuring that WC's branch will remain in operation.

WC's key gateway is Chicago. Since start-up, WC has added several trains to the North Fond du Lac-Chicago corridor. In May 1990, freight traffic had grown to the point that WC added a pair of trains to the three already operated between North Fond du Lac and Chicago. A new wayfreight that made a turn from Neenah to Stevens Point was also added. Part of its job was to move intermodal trailers to and from Chicago trains at Neenah.

In late 1991 WC took steps to further improve connections at Chicago by rerouting a pair of trains from Shops Yard directly to Conrail and CSX. WC train destinations at Chicago have included Soo's Schiller Park Yard, Burlington Northern's Cicero Yard, Belt Railway of Chicago's Clearing Yard, Chicago Central's Hawthorne Yard, CSX's Barr Yard, and Illinois Central's Markham Yard. Over the years, WC has changed Chicago terminals for several runs, particularly the intermodal trains, which have shifted from Union Pacific's Canal Street facility to Santa Fe's Corwith Yard, back to Canal Street, and then to Illinois Central at Harvey.

WC is constantly searching for ways to cut costs. Holding down track material costs can ultimately increase profit. One way WC has done this is to recycle track materials from abandoned lines. WC inherited several lines that were still intact even though Soo Line had received permission to abandon them. In its first few years WC pulled up 51 miles from Dresser to Danbury, Wis., 26 miles from Medford to Prentice, 16 miles from Almena to Amery, 8.8 miles from Chippewa Falls to Eau Claire, 7 miles from Wisconsin Rapids to Vesper, and a mile in Menasha. Three sections of the old DSS&A were pulled up: Sidnaw to Bergland, 45 miles, Trout Lake to St. Ignace, 27 miles, and Soo Junction (Ishpeming) to Humboldt Junction, Mich. (12 miles abandoned in favor of trackage rights over the parallel LS&I). Another 23 miles of DSS&A track, from Nestoria to Sidnaw, Mich., was sold to short line neighbor Escanaba & Lake Superior.

Unlike some railroads, which deliberately attempt to drive away customers so they can abandon lines, WC maintained a policy of not abandoning lines where any customers might remain. After trimming off the little-used or already abandoned lines in its early years, WC has concentrated on cutting back redundant parallel trackage, usually following the acquisition of new sections of railroad.

Recognizing that improving access to Canada could bring new business, WC concentrated on improving its link to that country at the Soo. A series of bridges linking the two cities of Sault Ste. Marie has been operated as the Sault Ste. Marie Bridge Company, a wholly owned subsidiary of Wisconsin Central Transportation Corporation since January 16, 1988, when WC purchased Canadian Pacific's share. While the bridge company is operated as

While most WC lines were in good condition at start-up, several needed work. Prime among these was the 44-mile branch from Neenah to Manitowoc. Soo Line let the line deteriorate to a 10 mph pace and had closed the portion west of Hilbert, where it crossed Soo's ex-Milwaukee Road line to Green Bay. WC reopened the line, and aided by a grant and low-interest loan from the Wisconsin Department of Transportation, upgraded it to 25 mph maximum speed. On May 7, 1990, tie replacement is in progress near Collins. After the acquisition of Fox River Valley, the branch became the primary conduit to reach both WC and ex-FRVR customers in Manitowoc.
— *Otto P. Dobnick*

Branch lines weren't the only part of the WC system to see upgrades. The portion of the railroad between North Fond du Lac and Chicago carries the largest volumes of traffic, and since start-up, speeds have been increased from 40 to 50 mph. Constant maintenance is in order to keep this "funnel" in top condition. Sperry Rail Service cars make routine visits to many WC lines, searching for possible rail defects. On June 12, 1993, train T219 passes Sperry car 129 waiting in the siding at Vernon, seven miles south of Waukesha. — *Gregory C. Sieren*

WC's link between the United States and Canada is the bridge spanning the St. Mary's River and Soo Locks between Sault Ste. Marie, Mich., and Ontario. Opened in 1888, the structure is owned by the Sault Ste. Marie Bridge Co., a subsidiary of Wisconsin Central Transportation Corporation and a separate Class 3 railroad. The distance from WC's yard in Sault Ste. Marie, Mich., to the Canadian shore is 1.2 miles, covered by 23 bridge spans. The oldest spans date from 1887 and the newest is the lift bridge over the Poe Lock on the U. S. side, opened in 1959, replacing a swing bridge built in 1899. On December 15, 1991, WC's daily transfer crosses the bridge as it returns from Canadian interchange duties with CP and ACR. This was a regular assignment for SDL39s, such as the 585. — *Dennis Pehoski*

part of WC, it is technically a separate Class 3 railroad, with its own reporting marks, SSAM.

The oldest spans of the bridge are pin-connected through trusses over the Canadian rapids that date from 1887. In 1991 WC strengthened the bridge by installing two new girder spans to accommodate 100-ton shipments. The bridge had been restricted to 89 tons, severely limiting the large diesel locomotives that could be used on it. The five-month project involved replacing two 104-foot pony truss spans over the power canal on the Canadian end of the bridge. The new spans were manufactured "next door" by Algoma Steel in Sault Ste. Marie, Ontario. The old spans were donated to the Sault Ste. Marie Waterfront Development Group to be used as footbridges. WC's 1995 acquisition of Algoma Central and the routing of more traffic between the Algoma Central and the United States have justified the strengthening of the bridge.

Eighty-seven miles west of Sault Ste. Marie, WC was able to capitalize on another opportunity to expand its business. For years, Inland Lime & Stone Co., a subsidiary of Inland Steel, operated a limestone mine near Gulliver, Mich. To move the limestone to a crusher at Port Inland, Mich., on Lake Michigan, the railroad used its own electric locomotives on a 7-mile private railroad. The line's only rail connection was at its remote bridge over WC's Gladstone-Sault Ste. Marie line.

In December 1989 Inland shut down the operation and mothballed the quarry, crusher, and railroad. In 1991 the property was purchased by Pfizer Specialty Minerals, Inc., which felt it could operate at a lower cost than Inland. Pfizer rehabilitated the property and set plans to reopen. Because the locomotives, cars, and track were in poor condition, Pfizer planned to purchase trucks to move the limestone. Wisconsin Central offered to rehabilitate the railroad and the car fleet if it could operate the line and convinced Pfizer that approach would be cheaper than buying and operating trucks. An agreement was signed, and WC engineering and mechanical department people went to work at Pfizer in early 1991. They reworked nearly 16 miles of track for 40 mph operation, installed 7,600 new ties, and refurbished Pfizer's fleet of 70 side-dump gondolas. Limited three-day-a-week operation began in May 1991, with daily operations resuming in 1992. The quarry and crusher operate during the Great Lakes navigation season, usually from April until freeze-up in November. Thanks to this aggressive pursuit of new business, WC was able to gain a new source of transportation revenue, and Pfizer gained a low-cost method of moving its raw limestone. The operation is now Calko Specialty Minerals, Inc.

Acquisition of new equipment was part of the strengthening of Wisconsin Central. In June 1989 the company placed its first order for new cars, 250 100-ton covered hoppers — $11 million worth — to carry roofing granules for customers at Kremlin, Mich., and Wausau, Wis. In early 1990 WC ordered 150 more at a cost of almost $7 million.

Car and roadway programs gave WC one of the most ambitious capital programs among regionals, totaling $20.4 million in 1990 — up from $17.7 million in 1989 and $9.6 million in 1988. In 1994 WC placed the largest single order for new cars by a modern regional railroad. It included 700 100-ton covered hoppers, 300 100-ton gondolas, and 50 extra-high 100-ton boxcars to handle 3-meter rolls of paper.

WC has made it a point to provide high-quality freight equipment for paper shipments, which are especially susceptible to damage. Over 6,600 cars were overhauled at Shops in WC's first seven years. At start-up, there were only 12 workers in the car shop, but by 1990 this had grown to 48, and by 1995, the North Fond du Lac shops employed 95 people in car rebuilding programs. The number of cars overhauled grew as well. Between 1987 and 1989 WC rebuilt 754 cars, then exceeded that figure in 1990, when 789 cars were put through the shop. 1993 was a banner year with 1,583 cars, and 700 cars were shopped in 1995.

Contracts from outside customers to repair cars and locomotives have helped WC achieve high utilization at the North Fond du Lac shops: repairs, painting, and modifications to freight cars for Soo Line, Southern Pacific, Union Tank Car Co., Bethlehem Steel, Johnstown America Corporation, and a Consolidated Papers affiliate. WC has performed locomotive work for Wisconsin & Southern, Metra (the Chicago commuter rail operator), Wisconsin industrials such as Flambeau Paper and A. O. Smith, and Oxford Group, Inc. The company has undertaken private passenger car refurbishing for Charter Manufacturing Company.

HUNGRY FOR BUSINESS

As representatives of a new railroad eager to achieve success, WC's marketing and operating people moved aggressively to attract new business that had left the rails because of poor service or lack of effort. In the early 1990s, intermodal traffic increased markedly on many Class 1 railroads but not on many regional railroads. WC was the exception. When it began operation in 1987, WC inherited a pair of overnight intermodal trains, 218 and 219, between Chicago and Green Bay. They had begun operation the year before as "Sprint" trains, and under the WC regime business expanded. In 1989 WC opened new intermodal ramps at Neenah and Stevens Point. In 1991 the Stevens Point facility was expanded to enable a mechanized "Piggypacker" to be used for loading. The same year an agreement was reached with Santa Fe establishing an integrated price and service package between WC intermodal points and destinations in Arizona and California. WC also began joint-marketing arrangements with BN America and CSX Intermodal, and connected with CN North America's intermodal services at Superior. In 1991 WC's total intermodal volume rose 37 percent over 1990 to 28,300 units. In 1993 this reached 31,710 units; in 1994, 42,595 units.

Not all intermodal ventures succeeded. On August 3, 1992, WC inaugurated a second pair of Chicago-Green Bay intermodal trains, T220 and T221, primarily to serve trucking giant J. B. Hunt. The trains were often short and were dropped in 1993 because of a shortage of power and crews caused by other business increases. The Hunt traffic, mostly sanitary paper made in Green Bay, was switched to T218 and T219. T220 and T221 returned to WC's timetables in 1994, when intermodal traffic increased.

WC has also been involved in a number of unusual traffic movements. In 1990 and 1991, the railroad moved loads of 36-inch pipe for the 460-mile Great Lakes Gas Transmission Co. pipeline then being constructed from Duluth across northern Wisconsin and both peninsulas of Michigan. Included in these moves was a trip over the 33-mile Mellen-Bessemer line that had remained unused during WC's early years. In 1991, shortline entrepreneur

Most Class 1 railroads gave up handling pulpwood traffic during the 1970s. WC, however, remains convinced that money can be made on pulpwood moves, even though they frequently involve moving a few cars at a time over relatively short distances. The traditional way of loading pulpwood logs into rail cars has changed little. In October 1988 a logger is loading a WC gondola at Glidden, Wis. WC has aggressively gone after the pulpwood business, and significant volumes of this traffic have returned to the Superior, Ashland, and Newberry Subs.
— *Brian Buchanan*

In May 1990 a pair of GP30s are rolling by the giant Weyerhaeuser mill at Rothschild with train L018. Behind the GP30s is a string of pulpwood loads, brought south the night before by L016 from Mellen. Pulpwood is among several commodities that make up paper industry traffic. Inbound shipments include wood chips, waste paper, clay and chemicals, and occasionally machinery, while outbound traffic includes paper, paperboard, wood pulp and lignin, a by-product. Many mills, including Weyerhaeuser, have their own switch engines to move cars around their plants.
— *Otto P. Dobnick*

Craig Burroughs announced plans to lease the line from WC to handle shipments of logs and iron ore. Dubbed the Wisconsin & Michigan Railroad, freight operations began June 12, 1992, and the next year tourist passenger service was offered using former LS&I GE U23C locomotives. Before the railroad began operations, Burroughs failed in an attempt to force WC, through a filing with the ICC, to sell him the White Pine Line. He planned to link up the line with the Bessemer trackage. The ICC rejected the application. Wisconsin & Michigan hauled a bit of freight, but didn't run its tourist trains in 1994 and ceased operations February 12, 1995. WC then moved to abandon this line.

Another unusual move by WC was hauling huge rocks for breakwater construction on flatcars from Valders to Manitowoc, only 12 miles. While most railroads would cringe at such a short haul, WC with its flexible crews and low costs was able to make money on the operation. Other rock shipments include the transport of crushed granite ballast from the Mathy Construction quarry south of Mosinee, Wis., to Chicago area railroads (the quarry is also WC's main ballast source). In the summer WC hauls unit trains of aggregates from quarries at Cedar Lake and Sussex, Wis., to northern Illinois for contractors who use the rock for highway and home construction.

Although it didn't seem so at the time, one of the most important developments to take place on the railroad occurred early in 1989, when WC and USX — formerly U. S. Steel — signed an agreement to move 12 trains of taconite pellets from Superior (Ambridge) to Chicago. The ore originated at USX's Minntac pellet plant near Mountain Iron, Minn., on the Duluth, Missabe & Iron Range Railway. At Chicago, WC handed it off to

Conrail for delivery to USX's Edgar Thompson Works in Pittsburgh. This was the first "all-rail" ore move handled by WC, and indeed was a harbinger. USX was so pleased that it contracted with WC to move 70 more trains to the Thompson Works in 1990. Since then the volume of ore has increased to the point that it is WC's largest type of traffic, measured in carloads.

Most marketing efforts were successful, but not all bore fruit. WC aggressively bid to move coal mined in Wyoming's Powder River Basin from connections in the Twin Cities to the Wisconsin Public Service Plant at Weston, south of Wausau. Ultimately the contract remained with Burlington Northern and Soo Line, although WC would garner a portion of this business a few years later. A scheme to develop a coal handling port in Manitowoc was shelved because of local concerns. Highway competition remains fierce. While WC carries substantial amounts of outbound heavy paper, most sheet and consumer paper products still go by truck to warehouses and retail stores.

NEIGHBORS

Wisconsin Central receives traffic from neighboring short lines as well as Class 1 railroads. Many of the smaller carriers are similar in style to WC, concentrating on personalized service and frequently operating on tracks cast off by larger railroads. One is Wisconsin & Southern (WSOR), which connects with WC at Slinger, Wis., and at Rugby Junction. WSOR originally began service on 147 miles of the Milwaukee Road's former Northern Division in July 1980 and expanded in August 1992 when it took over the Wisconsin & Calumet (WICT) west and south of Waukesha. After acquiring WICT, Wisconsin & Southern

The private railroad of Specialty Minerals Inc. carries limestone from quarries near Gulliver to Port Inland, Mich., where it is transferred to boats. Originally owned by Inland Lime & Stone Co., the operation was shut down in 1989, but reopened in 1991. WC persuaded the new owners that rebuilding the railroad and letting WC operate it to move limestone would be more cost-effective than trucks. A year after the mine reopened, SDL39 584 departs the quarry with a train of limestone for Port Inland. In 1995, WC handled over 5 million tons on this line. — *Steve Glischinski*

WC placed its first order for new equipment in 1989, when it purchased 250 100-ton covered hoppers to carry roofing granules, followed the next year by 150 more. In 1994 it placed orders for 1,050 new cars of various types, giving WC one of the largest fleet of new cars of any regional. On July 19, 1991 SDL39 586 is switching some of the new roofing granule hoppers at the GAF facility at Kremlin. — *Brian Buchanan*

66

In 1993 WC shops at Stevens Point and North Fond du Lac collaborated to build "remote-control" flatcars from three bulkhead flatcars. Car men at Shops removed one bulkhead from each car, installed railings and toe plates around the deck, and built walkways and stairs. Stevens Point shop forces installed remote-control equipment, a headlight, a five-chime horn, and light sets that indicate the various operating modes such as forward, reverse, and braking. The cars were built for use at the Specialty Minerals limestone quarry in Michigan, where they permit one-person operation and allow WC to rotate any locomotive in or out of mine operations. At Port Inland on May 6, 1993, WC engineer Daniel "Dale" Smith holds the remote-control box used to control the flatcar/locomotive. — *Steve Glischinski*

negotiated trackage rights over WC between Slinger and Waukesha to link its lines.

Another is the 14-mile Marinette, Tomahawk & Western Railroad. Founded in 1912 to serve lumber and paper mills, it connected Tomahawk on the Milwaukee Road, with Bradley, Wis., on the Soo Line. The WC uses trackage rights over the short line's main stem between Tomahawk and Bradley as part of its route from Wausau to Ashland, Wis. In 1991 MT&W was put up for sale by Tenneco, Inc. — parent company of Packaging Corporation of America (PCA), whose plant at Wisconsin Dam is the short line's largest shipper. WC bid to buy it, but Rail Management & Consulting Corporation of Panama City, Fla., was chosen on January 1, 1992. The new owners renamed the company Tomahawk Railway. It remains an independent carrier connecting exclusively with WC, which supplies equipment to Tomahawk.

WC connects with Escanaba & Lake Superior at Green Bay and Pembine, Wis., and North Escanaba, Mich. The E&LS, founded in 1897, originally operated only 70 miles of track, but expanded to 347 miles in 1980 when it acquired Milwaukee Road's lines from Green Bay to Ontonagon, Mich. E&LS serves paper mills in Ontonagon and Menominee and all of its interline traffic is interchanged with WC, primarily at Green Bay. In 1993, as a condition of support for WC's acquisition of Green Bay & Western and Fox River Valley, E&LS received trackage rights over WC from North Escanaba to Pembine, shorter and faster than E&LS's own line from Escanaba to Pembine via Channing.

Three other shortline connections are noteworthy. At Eagle Mills, Mich., WC interchanges with ore carrier Lake Superior & Ishpeming, owned by Cleveland Cliffs Iron Co. Formed in 1892, LS&I has shrunk to 44 miles. Almost all of its traffic consists of taconite from the Tilden and Empire mines to its Presque Isle dock at Marquette. Twin Cities switching road Minnesota Commercial (MNNR) is an important WC partner. WC uses a portion of the Commercial's yard in New Brighton for switching and coal train interchange and has trackage rights on MNNR into St. Paul. At Mukwonago, Wis., WC maintains an interchange with the 7-mile East Troy Electric Railroad, the last true electric interurban railway in the United States operating both freight and passenger service.

WC GOES PUBLIC

May 22, 1991, was Wisconsin Central's first day as a publicly held company. WC went public to raise funds to reduce the debt incurred to purchase the railroad. At the end of 1987, WC's debt-to-capital ratio was 91.1 percent. This was reduced somewhat in August 1989 when some of the high-interest debt was refinanced, thanks to WC's good financial position (WC paid off $15 million of debt in its first year). By the end of 1991, after the company went public, the debt-to-capital ratio had been reduced to 57 percent; in 1994 it was 35 percent. In the 1991 public sale, 2.4 million shares of common stock were sold,

netting $36.2 million. In 1992 a second stock offering brought in $48.7 million. This offering was intended to help finance the acquisition of the Green Bay & Western and Fox River Valley railroads, but when that purchase was delayed, WC used $35 million of the proceeds to further reduce debt. Employees were able to buy into a stock purchase plan, and those who did were happy — initially offered for $16.50 per share, the stock skyrocketed to over $60 per share by mid-1994, when directors approved a two-for-one stock split. A three-for-one split was approved in May 1996.

ALMOST A CLASS 1

Wisconsin Central must rely on its connecting Class 1 carriers to forward much of its traffic. WC has actively promoted good relationships with connections, although its relationship with Chicago & North Western was strained in 1992 when C&NW opposed WC's purchase of Fox River Valley, a 1988 C&NW spinoff. By early 1995, on the eve of North Western's absorption into Union Pacific, the two roads were on good terms again, with C&NW exercising its trackage rights option to operate from Superior to Necedah via a new connecting track at Junction City.

CP Rail's Soo Line is a regular visitor to WC rails, with coal trains utilizing trackage rights on the Valley Sub, and rock trains on the Dresser Sub. On several occasions, derailments or track work have forced Soo trains back to the main line through Stevens Point. Even Amtrak's *Empire Builder* has detoured over WC rails. Work stoppages and an Indian uprising in Canada caused CP to detour trains over WC from Sault Ste. Marie to Minneapolis.

One area where WC differs substantially from its Class 1 neighbors is in employment. Between 1987 and 1995,

Class 1 railroad employment declined 28 percent, but employment at WC doubled to a new high, 1,650.

Passenger service wasn't a part of WC's operating plan but the company has operated numerous passenger trains since start-up. Frequent specials were hosted by shipper Quad/Graphics, which has its own private cars, as well as tour operators Great Lakes Western and High Iron Travel Corp. Steam locomotive excursions have operated using Frisco 4-8-2 1522, Milwaukee Road 4-8-4 261, and C&NW 4-6-0 1385. Enthusiast groups such as the National Railway Historical Society and 20th Century Railroad Club have sponsored trips. Some have been keyed to local celebrations such as the Burlington (Wis.) Chocolate City Festival. WC has actively supported rail historical societies and museums in its territory through donations or by providing services.

To encourage grade-crossing safety, WC has sponsored trains for Operation Lifesaver, the rail industry's crossing safety program. In July 1991 WC operated a special train for judges, prosecuting attorneys, and chiefs of police — a video camera on the front of the locomotive let them observe motorists trying to beat the train to crossings.

WC maintains a modest fleet of passenger cars for special operations. Originally, WC leased two cars from private owners: former Milwaukee Road open platform business car *Prairie Rose* and ex-CB&Q open platform dome lounge *Sierra Hotel*. With the acquisition of GB&W in 1993 came the first WC-owned business car, ex-Union Pacific dome lounge *Trempealeau River*. With the Algoma Central acquisition WC gained heavyweight business cars *Agawa*, built in 1913, and *Michipicoten*, built in 1910.

Thanks to WC's healthy growth in revenues, it nearly was classified a Class 1 carrier, which would make it subject to more extensive and expensive rate and financial regulations. In 1991 railroads with annual revenues exceeding $90 million for three consecutive years were considered "Class 1" by the ICC, but that year the ICC granted requests from WC and Montana Rail Link to exempt them from Class 1 reporting requirements. Since then, the Class 1 revenue threshold has been increased, and WC remains a Class 2 railroad.

Since it began operations, WC has been a non-union company. It was a strong conviction of WC President Ed Burkhardt that there should be a close relationship between a successful company and its employees, and that unions destroy that relationship. In 1989 and 1990, the Brotherhood of Locomotive Engineers began a drive to organize WC operating personnel. Despite an intensive effort, employees overwhelmingly rejected the union. However, WC would hear from the unions again in 1992, when the railroad was in the midst of plans for route expansion.

C&NW's route to Superior was one of the few lines in Wisconsin it had overhauled in recent years. Welded rail was in place over much of it; WC added more, plus new ties and ballast. The new route sees heavy trains, particularly during winter when the all-rail ore season is in full swing. On November 6, 1994, train T004 is grinding up the 1 percent grade out of South Itasca yard amid a sun-filled snow squall, a regular occurrence in this area thanks to the presence of Lake Superior a few miles north. — *Robert C. Anderson*

5

EXPANSION AND ENHANCEMENT

THE SUPERIOR CONNECTION

Wisconsin Central came of age in the 1990s. Train service was reliable and on time. The locomotive fleet was dependable, and WC had built up an excellent fleet of new and rebuilt freight cars, thanks to the able shop forces at North Fond du Lac. Earnings remained on the increase, and more and more dollars were plowed back into the physical plant. The trade magazine *Railway Age* named WC its "Regional Railroad of the Year" in 1992 for setting "an example of prudent management and bold marketing for the entire industry." WC remained on the lookout for ways to expand its business and saw opportunities in the Twin Ports of Duluth and Superior.

WC hoped to access interchange traffic at the Twin Ports, especially the large volume of overhead traffic off the Duluth, Winnipeg & Pacific. However, handling overhead traffic was prohibited by WC's 1987 purchase agreement, since such moves could take business away from Soo Line. Soo retained the 102-mile line from Ladysmith

In 1993 WC employees at North Fond du Lac found a 56-inch steam locomotive driving wheel partially buried on the shop grounds. The wheel was dug out, refurbished, and put on display at the entrance to the diesel shop. The sign sums up the progress WC made in its first six years. — *Steve Glischinski*

to Superior, granting WC trackage rights only for local business, as a way to protect its bridge traffic out of the Twin Ports.

WC attempted to purchase Soo's "Ladysmith Line" in 1990, but the asking price was too high. Instead, WC turned to C&NW, which agreed to sell its lightly trafficked line out of Superior as far as Cameron, Wis., for $5.8 million. WC trains could run from Superior to Cameron on the North Western, then turn east onto WC at Cameron to reach Ladysmith. On December 18, 1990, C&NW and WC signed a letter of intent for the purchase; full ICC approval came on December 5, 1991. Included with the ICC filing was a request to abandon WC's own Cameron-Rice Lake branch, which paralleled the C&NW. As part of the deal, North Western acquired trackage rights over WC between Superior and Wisconsin Rapids via Ladysmith (it already had rights over WC between its main line at Necedah and Wisconsin Rapids). C&NW retained owner-ship of its branch from Trego to Hayward to serve a major industry there (WC purchased it in 1996).

However, WC never used the routing via Cameron. When WC reached agreement with C&NW, a clause in the original Soo purchase agreement kicked in. This clause stipulated that if WC acquired another route into Superior, Soo had the option to sell the Ladysmith line to WC, and WC was required to buy it at the same price it was paying for the other route. There were other legal maneu-verings over this issue, but ultimately Soo sold the line for $15.8 million. On August 8, 1991, WC applied to the ICC to purchase the Ladysmith line; the ICC approved it on November 5. On December 9, 1991, WC purchased the line and began accepting overhead shipments. Legal pro-ceedings held up the closing on the C&NW line until the following summer.

Rather than keep both lines, WC elected to combine the best parts of them. Both Soo and C&NW had steep grades out of Superior: 1 percent for 12 miles eastbound. However, the North Western line had welded rail, while Soo's line needed work. WC chose the C&NW route, and built a 2,047-foot connection on a 0.8 percent grade rising 18 feet to link the lines at Gordon, Wis.

At 11:39 a.m. on Thursday, July 9, 1992, WC and North Western signed the sale documents in Chicago. Upon receiving word of the closing, waiting crews began cutting into the C&NW welded rail at Gordon so a switch could be installed to make the connection. Work had begun in June, but workers could not physically tie the lines together until the agreement was signed. As crews worked at Gordon, train T004 began its journey at Superior, using the old Soo tracks for the last time July 9. As soon as it passed Gordon at 12:45 p.m., crews pulled up the rails, and bulldozers moved in to grade a path for the new connection. No trains ran through Gordon for 36 hours while crews worked furiously to complete the con-nection, which was termed "Trego Junction" but has since been renamed "Spur 422" for the milepost at Gordon (WC renumbered the mileposts on the C&NW line to in-tegrate it with the former Soo). The former Soo was aban-doned north of Gordon, as was the ex-C&NW from Gordon south to Rice Lake.

As the Gordon track was completed, C&NW crews were at work on another connection that allowed C&NW to access its branch to Hayward, which passed under WC at a point 20 miles south of Gordon. Dubbed "Hayward Junction," the new connection was opened on July 9. C&NW then utilized trackage rights from Superior to Hayward Junction to reach the branch.

The new routing gave WC the shortest route between the Twin Ports and Chicago — 461 miles, versus 562 miles for C&NW, 568 for Soo via Minneapolis, and 591 miles for BN. Now free to solicit through business out of Superior, WC entered into fierce bidding to land a contract for Canadian National "haulage" trains. This traffic, destined for Chicago, comes out of Canada to Superior on CN's

Duluth, Winnipeg & Pacific. Even though WC's route was shorter, CN announced on November 2, 1992, that the contract would go to Burlington Northern. Nevertheless, Wisconsin Central continued to aggressively solicit business out of Canada, opening its first off-line marketing office, in Vancouver, British Columbia, the same year. Its efforts bore fruit on April 1, 1996, when CN, WC, and CSX Intermodal began a new intermodal service between the eastern United States and western Canada. The railways dubbed the new service, which moves via Superior, Wis., "The Superior Connection."

WC viewed expansion of its system as a key to its long-term survival. While it had already enjoyed success, the company struggled with the problems of operating a system with low traffic density. In 1991, WC had less than one-fourth the revenue per mile of the average Class 1 railroad — and most Class 1s considered their densities too low. While WC had an operating ratio below 80 percent (percentage of revenue to expenses), the company still was not generating enough cash to fund the capital improvements necessary to keep the physical plant maintained and competitive. The more traffic that could be obtained, the more cash would be generated. Expansion of the system could generate that traffic.

GREEN BAY & WESTERN AND FOX RIVER VALLEY

Even as the new route to Superior was assembled, WC planned a wider expansion: the acquisition of two competing Wisconsin railroads, Green Bay & Western (GB&W) and Fox River Valley (FRVR). The former was over 100 years old, and the latter was a new regional spun off by C&NW in 1988. Included in the deal would be 14-mile GB&W subsidiary Ahnapee & Western, dormant

since 1986. All were owned by Itel Rail Corp. and came under common management in 1991. Itel had spent $8 million in December 1977 to purchase GB&W as a base for its per diem lease fleet of rail freight cars. Boxcars were surplus at the time because of overbuilding in the late 1970s, compounded by a recession in the early 1980s. Itel viewed GB&W as part of its car operations, but when traffic grew in the late 1980s and early 1990s the boxcar surplus vanished and Itel could utilize its entire car fleet without GB&W.

GB&W's earliest predecessor, the Green Bay & Lake Pepin Railway, was chartered in 1866 and began construction in 1869. The 211-mile line across Wisconsin from Green Bay to East Winona was completed in 1873, with a bridge over the Mississippi River to Winona, Minn., opened in 1891. (The bridge, unused for several years, was destroyed by a fire in 1989.) The Green Bay & Western name first appeared in 1896. In 1891 the 36-mile Kewaunee, Green Bay & Western completed a line from Green Bay to Kewaunee, on Lake Michigan's west shore. GB&W acquired control of KGB&W in 1897, but it remained a separate entity, with locomotives sub-lettered "KGB&W," until 1969.

Popularly known as the "Green Bay Route," the GB&W gained fame when the McGee family took charge in 1934. Homer McGee, a Texas-born railroader, transformed the company after years of neglect, turning it into a lean, well-respected operation. Passenger service ended in 1949, and dieselization was completed in 1950 with a fleet of Alco diesels. In 1962, Homer McGee turned the railroad over to his son, H. Weldon McGee, who ran the railroad until it was acquired by Itel.

GB&W specialized in "bridging" overhead traffic from

In the early 1970s, GB&W removed the attractive gray stripe from the center of its diesels in favor of a less-complicated, all-red scheme. Showing off the solid red are a pair of C424s as they hustle east through the Trempealeau River Valley near Dodge, Wis., on September 11, 1976. — *Steve Glischinski*

The Fox River Valley may have had a short life, but during its brief existence it offered a lot for fans of unusual and elderly diesels, if not for its investors. Witness this northbound freight at Van Dyne in May 1990. On the point is SD24 2402, one of two owned by the railroad, among the last unrebuilt SD24s operating anywhere. Next is RSD15 2407, one of six Alco "Alligators" acquired from LS&I through Itel neighbor GB&W; the majority of these units never turned a wheel on FRVR. Trailing is SD35 2500, a former Southern Railway unit and the only one of its kind on FRVR's roster. In addition, FRVR relied on rebuilt GP7s, 9s, 30s, and 35s acquired from C&NW at startup.
— Otto P. Dobnick

Fox River Valley didn't have a lot of cash to spend painting locomotives. Only four of its 31 units were ever painted in full FRVR red and yellow — the two SD24s by the supplying dealer and two GP9Rs by FRVR forces. Most FRVR units initially wore plastic signs that read "Fox River Valley Railroad, Green Bay, Wisconsin." When these began falling off, crude "FRV" letters were stenciled on. Repainted GP9R 1701 leads a westbound crossing College Avenue near downtown Appleton on December 5, 1992.
— Otto P. Dobnick

Winona to Kewaunee. From there freight cars were taken by carferries (owned by Ann Arbor and Chesapeake & Ohio) to Michigan railheads. This routing avoided the busy and delay-prone Chicago terminal. But routing decisions were dictated by rates, and with deregulation of rail rates coming in 1980, much of the cross-lake business was diverted by C&O-successor Chessie System away from the expensive ferries, which it hoped to abandon. GB&W gradually lost traffic. The last car ferry called at Kewaunee in November 1990, and GB&W had to rely even more on its on-line business, mainly paper-related industries at Green Bay and Wisconsin Rapids. Near the end, the railroad was not generating enough cash or spending enough on capital improvements to maintain its physical plant over the long term.

Things were worse at Fox River Valley Railroad. It carried a large debt right from start-up on December 9, 1988, when Itel paid C&NW $61 million for it. Operating cash flow was insufficient to service the debt, and Itel had to continually send cash to help it meet its obligations. FRVR's main line extended 127 miles from Milwaukee to Green Bay via Fond du Lac, plus a 50-mile branch line south from Green Bay to Manitowoc and Cleveland, Wis. Other branch lines included a dormant 18-mile line from Appleton to New London and a 9-mile line from Manitowoc to Two Rivers. An important revenue generator for FRVR was the 8-mile long Kimberly Subdivision along the Fox River from Appleton to "lower" Kaukauna, which serves two of the largest paper mills in the state.

The origin of FRVR's lines can be traced back to Chicago & North Western and its predecessors that had completed a line from Fond du Lac to Oshkosh, Appleton, and Fort Howard (now Green Bay) between 1859 and 1862. In 1873 a connection between Fond du Lac and Milwaukee was completed, providing C&NW with its first Green Bay-Milwaukee route, which came to be known as the "Valley Line." A parallel route, the "Lake Shore Line," was born when a line from Milwaukee to Sheboygan, Manitowoc, Two Rivers, Appleton, and New London was constructed between 1873 and 1876. The gap from Manitowoc to Green Bay was closed in 1906. All these components were folded into C&NW, and in 1988, they were sold to FRVR — with one exception. The line from Milwaukee to Sheboygan was retained by C&NW because it served a coal-fired power plant at Sheboygan. C&NW kept ownership to Cleveland, Wis., 12 miles north of Sheboygan.

North Western originally intended to sell the lines from Duck Creek, north of Green Bay, to Escanaba and Ishpeming to another operator, but the "Duck Creek North" lines were ultimately retained and became an isolated C&NW operation after the FRVR spin-off. In 1996 Union Pacific put them up for sale again, and WC was the winning bidder on them.

By 1991 Itel decided its two marginal railroads had to go, and approached Wisconsin Central. Discussions took place in secrecy, and on January 8, 1992, Wisconsin Central Transportation Corp. announced it was forming a new subsidiary, Fox Valley & Western Ltd. (FV&W), to acquire the two railroads. GB&W was priced at $8.4 million, FRVR $52.8 million.

The announcement came as a surprise to C&NW and to rail labor. Their response was immediate: C&NW lashed out, claiming the acquisition would result in a "monopoly" for WC — despite the fact that trucks had taken over much of the rail traffic in the previous decade.

North Western painted itself as the friend of the shipper, the state, and local communities — conveniently leaving out that it had reduced service, allowed track to deteriorate, and abandoned hundreds of miles of lines throughout Wisconsin during the previous two decades. When it sold the FRVR trackage to Itel, North Western built in interchange restrictions that assured it of receiving the majority of the new railroad's business. Now most of that business would go to WC, and C&NW adamantly opposed WC's bid. C&NW, along with CP Rail's Soo Line, requested that the ICC put far-reaching conditions on the sale so they could retain traffic. Organized labor also opposed the sale, recognizing the loss of membership that would result from a non-union FV&W (GB&W was unionized, FRVR was not).

Final briefs were filed with the ICC on September 25, 1992, and on December 10, the sale was approved with no traffic conditions imposed. Although opposing railroads lost, labor gained a partial victory when the ICC ordered that protective conditions under its New York Dock ruling be imposed for any employees not offered jobs as a result of the transaction. New York Dock dictated that employees receive compensation if they lost their jobs — a condition WC was willing to live with. It was the first time the ICC had ever imposed employee protective conditions on a new start-up regional.

Start-up was expected by the end of 1992, but it was not to be, for labor gained partial late victories. Around this time FRVR employees voted for union representation on their railroad. Then, after reviewing arguments from rail labor organizations, the Commission issued a new order on January 25, 1993. This order required FV&W, along with FRVR/GB&W management, to negotiate implementing agreements with employees or their representatives to comply with the New York Dock conditions. Putting these agreements together turned out to be a lengthy task as arbitrators working with the two sides hammered out the agreements. Negotiations dragged on into summer, and the last arbitration ruling came in at noon on Friday, August 27, 1993. With the implementing agreements in place, WC was free to close the deal — which it did that day.

Unlike WC's start-up six years earlier, FV&W's first day went smoothly, since plans had been in place for months to ease the transition. As soon as the closing paperwork was signed in Chicago, start-up information was mailed to customers. As the last GB&W and FRVR trains arrived at their nearest terminals, the railroads shut down. Shipment information was loaded into WC's Transportation Control System at the Customer Service Center in Stevens Point — and this time none was lost. Engineering employees checked tracks, bridges, and buildings and installed new switch locks. Radio towers, which had already been set up, were placed in service. A new North Desk dispatching position was inaugurated at Stevens Point, staffed by six former GB&W/FRVR dispatchers. The first FV&W train rolled at 5 a.m. on Saturday, August 28, 1993, when engineer George Marino and conductors Larry Lins and Eddie Geiger came to work on FL091, a Neenah-Combined Locks turn on the lucrative Kimberly Sub. Mainline trains started running that afternoon.

For its money WC received 479 miles of railroad, 53 locomotives (including 22 Alcos), and 1,275 freight cars. In the Fox Valley area alone, the new railroad added nearly 100 new customers to WC's traffic base, which

The main lines of Fox River Valley and WC were parallel most of the way between Appleton and North Fond du Lac. In preparation for the FV&W purchase, WC planned to construct eight connecting tracks between the two lines; many were complete prior to start-up, and soon the railroad realized the necessity of a ninth crossover south of Oshkosh. New connections allowed trains to move from FV&W to WC south of Appleton, and connected FV&W and WC's Shops Yard in five locations at North Fond du Lac. At Oshkosh, two connections permit WC trains to use the FV&W main through the city. On September 6, 1994, train T008 led by SD45 6505, waits for train T001 to clear at Black Wolf, south of Oshkosh. Once No. 1 clears, No. 8 will use the connecting track to return to the WC main. — *Jeff Hampton*

Because WC does not own a yard in Chicago, its freights and transfers navigate the switching district's labyrinth of trackage to reach other carriers' yards. Wisconsin Central is a major user of Belt Railway of Chicago's facilities. On March 5, 1994, train 42 from Shops has arrived at BRC's Clearing Yard behind SD45s 6524 and 6584. BRC GP38-2s are clearing out a track in the west receiving yard to allow No. 42 to double its train into the yard. — *Brian Buchanan*

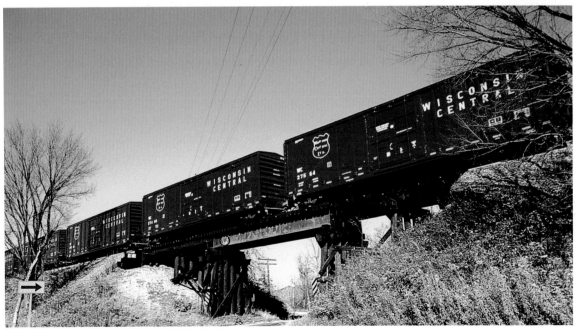

Since it hauls so much paper and paper-related products, WC needs high-quality boxcars. When the railroad was created, it purchased 2,900 cars from Soo Line, most of which were rebuilt at North Fond du Lac. Rebuild efforts on "paper" boxes include installation of smooth end linings, gas-filled end-of-car cushioning units, and rebuilt trucks. By the end of 1995, Shops had rebuilt or modified approximately 6,600 cars. "We spend more on equipment, for a railroad our size, than any other railroad in the country," WC president Burkhardt said in 1995. Fresh out of North Fond du Lac, a string of rebuilt boxcars rolls above Wildlife Road south of Allenton, Wis., on October 27, 1994. — *J. David Ingles*

caused an immediate increase in traffic and trains. For example, there were eight WC assignments at Neenah prior to FV&W; after start-up there were 20. Other new service included a Green Bay-Stevens Point train via Neenah. Since there is no direct connection between the Green Bay and Stevens Point lines at Neenah, the train operated with a locomotive at each end so that crews could switch ends instead of running locomotives around the train. Concurrent with the growth in traffic, mainline trains T050 and T051 were added between North Fond du Lac and Norfolk Southern's Calumet Yard in Chicago.

WC had anticipated a traffic upsurge and advanced several projects to increase capacity. At Stevens Point, two yard tracks were lengthened, while at Neenah two new tracks were constructed. An old connection was reinstalled between the WC and ex-GB&W mains at Amherst Junction, to preserve service to an important agricultural shipper at Amherst Jct. This permitted salvage of the unused Plover-Scandinavia segment, the only major piece of GB&W planned to be dismantled because of the acquisition.

For 33 miles between Appleton and North Fond du Lac, the WC and former FRVR mains were parallel, often within a few hundred feet of each other, and WC saw opportunities galore for economizing. In this stretch WC built nine connecting tracks to link the mains, many of them prior to start-up. This allowed the abandonment of the parallel FRVR line between Neenah and Oshkosh.

WC had plans for removing other short segments as well. Five connections in the North Fond du Lac area allowed trains to transfer between the WC and ex-FRVR yards. In addition to connections, WC made important improvements at Shops Yard. They included a $20 million, three-year project to convert the former FRVR yard to a westbound classification and ore train inspection facility, and reconfiguring the WC yard for eastbound classification. Even the old FRVR yard office was recycled; it was remodeled to house the WC/FV&W human resources office.

Green Bay, which went from five to three railroads overnight, saw the most change. The large North Green Bay yard, which had been the major C&NW and later FRVR facility, became the nucleus of FV&W operations. Since it had plenty of capacity, WC removed excess trackage at its ex-Milwaukee Road Oakland Avenue Yard. This allowed additional space for the intermodal terminal that remained at Oakland. Tracks were rebuilt and connected to the FV&W main, permitting the removal of the former Milwaukee/C&NW Tavil crossing. GB&W's Norwood Yard was closed and used for car storage.

The old FRVR line from Green Bay to Appleton, once laced with 10-mph slow orders, was quickly upgraded to allow 49-mph operation. On October 27, 1993, the city of Oshkosh and WC ratified an agreement to remove the former Soo Line tracks through the city, eliminating 40 grade crossings, mainly on Division Street, where the tracks ran down the street. The FV&W main was extensively upgraded with welded rail and CTC, financed with a loan from Wisconsin's Rail Capital Infrastructure Fund. The last train, a passenger special commemorating the end of service of the line, rolled down Division Street on January 27, 1996. In 1995, the use of the Fox Valley & Western name was dropped from marketing efforts in favor of Wisconsin Central in an effort to simplify the company's public image.

October 31, 1992, was a red-letter day for WC. On that date President George Bush, campaigning for re-election, rode WC rails from Burlington to Chippewa Falls. The 18-car special, powered by a specially painted CSX C40-8 locomotive, carried the president, his staff, and members of the news media. Tim Kelly, WC's assistant vice president–transportation, developed the operating plan for the train and coordinated operations with the U. S. Secret Service. Handling the "POTUS" (President Of The United States) special required a tremendous amount of coordination: a pilot train had to run ahead of the POTUS special, and two diesel units ran behind in case a reverse move was necessary. The move went flawlessly, although Bush was defeated in the November election. — *Otto P. Dobnick*

President Bush wasn't the only politician to campaign via WC. In 1990, Wisconsin Governor Tommy Thompson rode a three-car whistle-stop special from Burlington to Green Bay. On November 3, the "Governor Thompson Victory Express" stops for some speech-making at Waukesha as the Governor uses the back platform of leased WC business car *Prairie Rose* in classic campaign fashion. The train helped secure a third term for the governor. — *Otto P. Dobnick*

Even after FV&W began operations, the United Transportation Union made an aggressive drive to unionize WC operating crews, anxious to recapture members it had lost and seeing an opportunity for growth. The union asked employees to sign "A" cards to require a vote on union representation. Thirty five percent of engineers or conductors had to sign cards, and enough were accumulated to call for an election. WC gained a major victory when the National Mediation Board (NMB) allowed WC and FV&W to be considered one system for voting purposes. After lengthy delays, operating employees voted in fall 1994. On November 9, the NMB announced that 26 percent of the locomotive engineers and 37 percent of the conductors on the two railroads had voted in favor of the union. Since 50 percent was required to gain representation, the union went down to defeat. WC operating crews turned down a similar bid from the Brotherhood of Locomotive Engineers in 1990, with 21 percent of engineers and 15 percent of trainmen in favor. For WC management one troubling aspect of the vote was that the percentage in favor of union representation had crept upward from 1990.

Employees rejected union representation for a variety of reasons, among them possible loss of profit-sharing and 401(k) retirement plans. But a bigger factor probably was that many WC operating employees, having already experienced operations on unionized railroads, were anxious to "railroad" in an open, nonrestrictive environment. All of this took place while WC/FV&W employment had risen to an all-time high of 1,650 — a number that exceeded the levels of employment of all three previous owners of WC properties. While WC won this battle, it was certain that labor would return for another round.

NEW ZEALAND RAIL LIMITED

WC expansion efforts weren't limited to the United States. On July 20, 1993, WC announced the formation of yet another subsidiary, Wisconsin Central International (WCI), to acquire a stock interest in New Zealand Rail Limited (NZR), which was being privatized by the New Zealand government. The 2,500-mile, 3-foot 6-inch gauge NZR system serves all the principal commercial centers and seaports in New Zealand and is the only rail service in this Pacific island nation. NZR in 1993 had 5,300 employees, 269 locomotives and 6,000 freight cars and carried a variety of commodities including steel, timber, forest products, pulp, paper, coal, meat, wool, dairy products, and intermodal traffic. NZR provides long-distance passenger service, commuter service in Auckland and Wellington, and commercial ferry service linking New Zealand's north and south islands.

A consortium of investors was put together to purchase the railroad. WCI made a $16 million equity investment, for which it received a 27 percent interest. As part of WC's involvement, Burkhardt was named Chairman of NZR's board of directors. WC also has a contract to provide management services to NZR and sent John Bradshaw, WC's Vice President-Transportation, to New Zealand where he served as NZR's Group General Manager–Operations. Since 1993, NZR and WC have made frequent exchanges of technology and personnel. For example, downsizing led to an excess of locomotive engineers in New Zealand, while WC had a shortage. After a careful screening process, 10 NZ Rail engineers were picked from 190 applicants to travel to Wisconsin for a three-year stint with WC starting in 1995. Also in 1995, NZR changed its name to Tranz Rail Limited.

ALGOMA CENTRAL

Another international expansion, but closer to home, took place in January 1995 when WC acquired the 321-mile Canadian regional Algoma Central Railway (ACR). Running through rugged wilderness from Sault Ste. Marie to Hearst, Ontario, ACR had been in business for 95 years. A new Canadian WC subsidiary, WC Canada Holdings, was established for the acquisition. The railway is operated under the name Algoma Central Railway Inc. (ACRI).

Chartered as the Algoma Central Railway Company, ACR was incorporated August 11, 1899. Its builders hoped to reach Hudson Bay, so in 1901 the name was changed to Algoma Central & Hudson Bay Railway Company. This goal was never achieved, and the name reverted to ACR in 1965. ACR was constructed in segments. By 1903, 56 miles of line had been built from Sault Ste. Marie north. An isolated branch line was opened from Helen Mine (about 140 miles north of the Soo) to Michipicoten on Lake Superior. By the end of 1911, the railroad had crossed the Montreal River, 92 miles north of the Soo, and track was extended from Helen Mine east to Hawk Junction and north 30 miles to Franz, a connection with Canadian Pacific. In 1912, the two sections were joined when the line from the Soo reached Hawk Junction. The railroad was completed from Franz to Hearst, 296 miles from Sault Ste. Marie, in 1914.

ACRI connects with CN's main line at Oba, CP's main at Franz, and the provincially owned Ontario Northland Railway (ONR) at Hearst. Between Franz and Oba, unique "floating" bridges span Squaw Bay and Hoodoo Bay, both part of Oba Lake. These bridges are supported by wood pilings driven deep into the bottomless northern muskeg. Algoma Central has one branch, the 26-mile Michipicoten Subdivision from Hawk Junction to Wawa and Michipicoten Harbor on Lake Superior. Sintered iron ore mined at Wawa is shipped to the railroad's biggest customer, Algoma Steel, at the Soo.

Algoma Central is most famous for its tourist passenger trains, which began operating in 1952 to scenic Agawa Canyon, sometimes called the "Grand Canyon of the East." The railway also provides local passenger service, the last south of Alaska that calls at wilderness flag stops for residents. Trains 1 and 2 operate between the Soo and Hearst three days a week in winter and six days a week in the warm weather months. This service is subsidized by the Ontario government. Just prior to the WC purchase, Algoma Central completed refurbishing its passenger cars — still steam-heated, almost the last on the continent.

Algoma Central's operating base is Steelton Yard, adjacent to the huge Algoma Steel complex in the Sault Ste. Marie, Ont. (the two firms are not related). ACRI dispatchers there control the entire railroad by Occupancy Control System (OCS) warrants. Until the WC purchase, the shop at Steelton maintained ACR's locomotives and cars. It now concentrates on lighter repair, and North Fond du Lac handles heavier work.

WC Canada Holdings acquired only the railway operations from ACC for approximately $8.4 million. The Province of Ontario, through the Northern Ontario Heritage Fund Corporation, provided a $4.8 million grant, a $2.9 million long-term interest-free loan, and a $700,000 nonvoting preferred stock investment in the new railway. Included in the sale was the right to use Algoma Central's Black Bear herald, which also remains in use by ACC on its boats. ACR's 23 locomotives and 966 cars were acquired by WCL Railcars for $11.3 million. WC

Renumbering all 23 of Algoma Central's EMD locomotives began at Steelton Shop on the afternoon of January 31, 1995. The old ACR number on each side was covered with maroon paint. New number-boards, shipped from Wisconsin, were inserted on the front, and WC shield decals were affixed to the front and rear of each locomotive. Mechanic Lin Shackleton applies a WC emblem to GP7 158 (soon to be 1506) that night. By the end of the next day, all ACR locomotives were renumbered. — *Steve Glischinski*

To release Algoma Central's GP38-2s and SD40-2s for freight ser-vice — they would be the youngest power on WC — Nadrowski searched for appropriate passenger power, and acquired a single FP7, six FP9s, and four F9B units from VIA Rail Canada. Returning from Hearst on its maiden trip, FP9 1751 (ex-CN/VIA 6506) flies around a curve with No. 2 on July 20 — the GP7 behind the F was along "just in case." Train crews, who had worked only with hood units, didn't like the Fs at first, but quickly came to enjoy the visibility afforded by the high-riding cab units. "They ride like Cadillacs," said one crew member. — *Steve Glischinski*

WC became an international corporation when it acquired an interest in New Zealand Rail (now Tranz Rail) in 1993. Tranz Rail operates passenger and freight trains through rugged mountain territory on 2,500 miles of 3-foot 6-inch gauge track. At Kaikoura on November 1, 1986, a southbound freight led by General Motors of Canada DF class 6093 is in the siding waiting for the northbound *Coastal Pacific,* en route from Christchurch to Picton on New Zealand's south island. This line lies between the coastal Kaikoura mountains and the Pacific coast and includes 21 tunnels along its 349-kilometer route. At Picton passengers can transfer to Tranz Rail ferries to travel to the more populous north island. — *Eric Walsh, Collection of Tom Hoffmann*

Wisconsin Central expanded into the United Kingdom early in 1996 when subsidiary Wisconsin Central International acquired stock ownership of the Rail Express System, Ltd. (RES) from the British government. The principal activity of RES is carrying the Royal Mail for the British Post Office. Christmas mail doubtless forms a large part of the contents of the sacks being loaded aboard the London King's Cross-to-Edinburgh *Capitals Mail* at Peterborough on December 14, 1995. — *Mel Holley/Rail Magazine*

Canada Holdings also purchased ACR's communication system, maintenance and shop equipment, inventory, and miscellaneous assets for $4.7 million.

The ACR acquisition was a first for WC on two fronts. First, it is WC's first unionized operation: WC came to agreement with all nine labor organizations that represented ACR employees, but the package virtually duplicates the company's non-union U. S. operations. Second, Wisconsin Central entered the scheduled passenger train business and is operating its major service, the Agawa Canyon tour train, without government subsidies. To pull the passenger trains, 11 F-units were purchased from VIA, with seven entering service during summer 1995. Their purchase freed other locomotives for freight operations in the United States and Canada. They are the only units lettered for Algoma Central.

GREAT BRITAIN

Wisconsin Central added a fourth country to its rail "empire" late in 1995. On December 11, 1995, Wisconsin Central Transportation Corporation announced that it had put together a consortium to acquire stock ownership of Great Britain's Rail Express Systems Limited (RES). The principal activity of RES is the carriage of letters for the Royal Mail, a division of the British Post Office. To acquire RES, WCTC put together a consortium that included its Wisconsin Central International (WCI) subsidiary, Berkshire Partners, a U. S. investment firm that helped found WCTC, and Fay Richwhite & Co., Ltd., a New Zealand investment firm that helped with the Tranz Rail acquisition. Each of the companies owns one third of the railroad's common stock; Ed Burkhardt is chairman of the RES board of directors.

On January 12, 1996, North & South Railways Limited, another consortium led by WCTC, was selected as the purchaser of British Rail's three trainload freight companies. The three companies, Loadhaul, Mainline, and Transrail, collectively haul bulk commodities throughout Great Britain and had 7,000 employees, 910 locomotives, and 19,300 freight cars at the time of the acquisition. The three companies were merged and are operated as English Welsh & Scottish Railway Ltd. (EW&SRL). Ed Burkhardt became chairman of the merged company.

CONTINUED EXPANSION

While WC's physical expansion continued, so did the search for more business. Coal traffic came to WC in the form of a deal with Wisconsin Public Service (WPS). Contracts between WPS and WC cover two-thirds of WPS's business, specifically all the coal destined to Pulliam station at Green Bay and about 60 percent of what is consumed at the Weston 1 and 2 plant south of Wausau. The contract, signed in 1992, extends to 2012. Weston 3 is supplied under three contracts. One contract for 900,000 tons handled by WC expired in 1995, but was renegotiated. The other two for 400,000 tons each were held by CP Rail's Soo Line, but were not due for renewal until the year 2000. All the coal comes from the Powder River Basin by either Burlington Northern Santa Fe or Union Pacific.

More new business came to WC with the opening of the Flambeau Mine in Ladysmith, Wis. A subsidiary of Kennecott Corp., the mine opened in 1993 and produces copper and gold extracted from a small open-pit mine. WC built a 1.6-mile spur to serve the facility, which ships an average of 13 cars a day to locations on the Ontario Northland in Quebec and Ontario. A total of

4,841 carloads were handled in 1994. At about the same time the Ladysmith mine opened, WC handled its one-millionth rail shipment — a carload of printing paper shipped from Mead Paper in Groos, Mich., on June 8, 1993 — quite a milestone for a company less than six years old at the time.

The future may bring more milestones for the young company. Nearly all Tranz Rail trains use one-person train crews, and this concept was introduced on WC road trains in 1995. Three ex-Algoma Central cabooses were modified with remote-control gear similar to the flatcars used at the Specialty Minerals operation. When the cabooses are coupled to a locomotive it becomes capable of being remotely controlled. The White Pine Line was the first with one-person crews. On arrival at White Pine, the engineer would use remote control to switch the plant and yard. WC plans a wider application of one-person crews on certain road trains that have little or no intermediate switching, usually in CTC territory.

The application of one-person crews became entangled in safety issues as a result of a catastrophic derailment in Weyauwega, Wis. At 5:55 a.m., March 4, 1996, Train L022 derailed in the center of town. Thirty-four cars left the rails; fourteen of them carried liquefied petroleum gas (LPG), and two of those were punctured in the derailment and ignited. The town of 1,700 had to be evacuated because of the threat of explosion.

WC put its emergency plan into effect immediately. Motels and hotels were reserved for residents, a command post was set up, and technicians were brought in to evaluate the burning wreckage. WC's Mechanical Superintendent–Cars Terry Corson, who had received training in handling emergencies, served as operations manager.

Newspapers across the country picked up the story. While some articles were critical of WC's safety record, in general the company received high marks for taking responsibility for the accident: the railroad paid all the expenses incurred by residents as a result of the derailment and evacuation, it paid nearly $400,000 to the Red Cross and the Salvation Army, it assembled professional teams to inspect houses and businesses, and it paid the repair costs.

On August 19, 1996, just before the railroad reached its ninth anniversary, Metra, the Chicago commuter railroad, began operating four weekday passenger trains each way between Antioch, Ill., and Franklin Park, where they switch to the former Milwaukee Road for the trips to and from Chicago Union Station. The North Central Service, as it is called, is Chicago's first new rail commuter service since 1928. While the passenger trains add traffic to the line, the improvements that they necessitated — a new CTC system, five lengthened passing sidings, and improved protection at 69 highway and street crossings — also increase the freight capacity of the busy Chicago-North Fond du Lac "funnel."

The 1995 sale of the Chicago & North Western to Union Pacific offered more expansion opportunities. In 1996 WC purchased two isolated UP segments: the Trego-Hayward branch and terminal trackage in the Wausau area. WC also won the bidding for the "Duck Creek North" ore lines. In any case, as long as WC keeps working toward its mission ". . . to offer superior transportation consisting of more frequent, dependable train service at competitive prices with proper equipment accomplished by customer minded employees," then chances are excellent that Wisconsin Central will continue to be a railroad success story into the 21st Century.

The rehabilitation and reopening of the line between Ladysmith and Prentice was a precursor of much more tonnage after Inland Steel and WC signed a three-year agreement for more Escanaba ore moves. On February 10, 1995, SD45s 6577 and 6594 and recently acquired AT&SF F45 5972 kick up the snow at Hawkins, Wis., with a loaded ore train for Escanaba. The old C&NW ore cars were back for a return engagement, requiring a special FRA waiver of interchange rules because of their age. To the right is evidence of renewed pulpwood loading. In 1993 WC also began moving gold and silver ore over this line from the Flambeau Mine at Ladysmith. — *Mike Cleary*

6

"DISPATCHER TO THE ORE TRAIN!"

IN THE BEGINNING

In February 1989, these were the only words needed for a Wisconsin Central dispatcher in Stevens Point to contact a 100-car unit train loaded with taconite — iron ore pellets — rumbling through central Wisconsin from Minnesota's Mesabi Range. The emphasis on the singular train was not unintentional since there was usually only one ore train moving on the WC at a time. In one of the many success stories surrounding Wisconsin Central's quest for new traffic, this would soon not be the case.

During the start-up years of 1987 and 1988, iron ore was unheard of on the new WC. After all, heavy 100-car unit trains were reserved for the large Class 1 railroads, not regional carriers that were supposed to be moving freight cars for local customers. That changed in early 1989. Although other types of ore, including copper, gold, and silver, are handled, it is taconite that has become a major commodity for WC.

Most taconite moves on WC originated at the USX Minntac plant near Mountain Iron, Minn., although there have been some exceptions. Eight trains operated for Armco in January and February of 1994 were loaded at Eveleth Mines' Fairlane plant near Forbes, Minn. On February 24, three WC SD45s were leading an Armco train through the Fairlane loader prior to beginning the trip down DM&IR, WC, and CSX to Middletown, Ohio. — *Robert C. Anderson*

89

A significant volume of overhead traffic has always traveled between Duluth and Chicago. In the early 1960s and 1970s, much of this tonnage was seasonal iron ore movements. Soo Line moved ore trains from the DM&IR at Ambridge, near Superior, to the Norfolk & Western at Chicago for forwarding to Granite City, Illinois. Back then, power for ore trains were lash-ups of GP9s and F7s. But this business largely disappeared in the 1970s.

Heavy demand by U. S. Steel (USX) during the winter, when the Great Lakes are closed to shipping, again resulted in the need for all-rail moves of taconite during the 1988–1989 season. The ore would originate at the Minntac pellet plant — the largest such plant in North America — near Mountain Iron, Minn. When Soo Line decided not to compete for this traffic, it allowed WC to handle it by special agreement on a per car royalty basis. In February and March of 1989, Wisconsin Central moved 1,222 carloads of taconite pellets in 12 trains from the DM&IR at Ambridge, Wisconsin, near Superior, to Conrail in Chicago. Eleven of the trains were destined for the Edgar Thompson Works in Pittsburgh, Pennsylvania, and one train was for Gary, Indiana.

Traditionally, iron ore and taconite from the Lake Superior ranges were hauled in specially built ore cars — ore jennies — unique to the area. These short, stocky, cars can be troublesome to handle and are known to be rough on track. Most of these little cars are 40 to 50 years old, in some cases requiring a waiver from the Federal Railroad Administration to be interchanged off home rails. As a result, for the first ore trains in 1989, WC worked with Conrail to supply standard 100-ton open-top hopper cars. Eventually, WC would acquire its own sizable fleet of conventional hopper cars for its expanding ore business.

The new Wisconsin Central wanted to show it was up to the job for these loads. In an oft-told story about the first ore train season, WC car inspectors discovered that the first train of hopper cars to be used arrived at Stevens Point with coal frozen in them. Rather than return the cars and risk starting off the relationship with USX badly, 58 WC people from several departments climbed into the cars with picks and sledge hammers to clean them out. In March, additional sets of hopper cars required cleaning, still one of the dirtiest jobs in railroading.

The first seasonal ore moves were a success for WC. USX was obviously pleased, because the traffic repeated during the winter of 1989 and 1990, as WC moved 6,600 more cars in 70 trains. Unit trains of taconite were not anticipated in the original business plan for the railroad, so this traffic was like icing on WC's revenue cake.

The ore trains were the heaviest trains handled by WC up to that time, requiring pusher engines leaving both Superior and Shops Yard. In Soo Line days, pushers on trains up the South Range out of Superior and up Byron Hill out of Fond du Lac were common, but except for the ore moves, WC trains have not regularly required helpers.

MORE ORE TRAINS

Traditionally, the economics of transporting iron ore dictated that shipments from Minnesota and Michigan to steel mills in the Midwest and East be handled by giant boats on the Great Lakes. Railroads handled the ore from the mines to the docks for loading into boats. In the past when the Great Lakes ports and locks froze over during winter, the mines either shut down or stockpiled ore at the lakehead until spring. The railroad industry's ability to handle iron ore on an all-rail basis was assisted by the development of economic taconite processing methods and plants in the 1950s and 1960s. Unlike natural ore, which has a mudlike consistency and freezes easily, taconite is a hard rock. The raw taconite ore is processed at plants near the mines into hard marblelike pellets. The pellets don't freeze as easily and are easier to transport and unload. Almost all iron ore mined in the United States today is taconite.

Perhaps the major reason for WC's success with taconite is that the WC main lines are well situated to take advantage of the natural flow of U. S. iron ore from the mines on the Mesabi range in northern Minnesota to steel mills located east and south of Chicago. WC also serves the Marquette range in Michigan's Upper Peninsula, the other major active iron ore range in the United States.

The WC route from Duluth-Superior to Chicago is almost 120 miles shorter than Burlington Northern Santa Fe's, the only other intact rail route in this corridor. Unlike the BN route, WC avoids the congestion of the Minneapolis-St. Paul terminal area. Given WC's labor cost structure and aggressive marketing, this routing has been good for the regional. Between 1994 and 1996, the railroad placed advertisements in mining industry trade publications encouraging steel producers to "Ship ore year-round" for "all-rail cost savings." The ads also emphasized reduced losses from fewer transloadings between boats, conveyor belts, and railroad cars.

Starting in 1990, ore traffic took off with a series of annual or multiyear contracts. First, USX opted to have more ore delivered to the Edgar Thompson mill using the same DM&IR-WC-CR routing during the 1990, 1991, and 1992 winter seasons. Then WC landed the first large contract. In March 1992 the railroad put together a successful one-year deal for 180 trains from the Minntac facility to the USX Fairfield mill near Birmingham, Alabama. Incredibly, the bid was assembled in less than seven hours! Among other logistics, WC personnel completed negotiations with two other railroads, and arranged for a fleet of 500 100-ton hopper cars to carry the pellets. The first train was loaded on April 4, 1992, only eight days after the bid was submitted. Following completion of this contract, USX extended it from 1993 through 1995.

WC has also operated several special one-time iron ore moves. The first was perhaps the most unusual. In November 1990, WC — in cooperation with DM&IR and C&NW — moved 2,200 carloads of ore for Inland Steel when Inland's regular suppliers in Michigan went on strike. Using traditional ore jennies, the trains originated at Inland's Minorca pellet plant near Virginia, Minn. DM&IR brought the trains to Superior, where C&NW took over for the move to Cameron, Wis. The trains were handed off to WC for the move east, to tiny Hermansville, Mich., where they returned to C&NW for movement to Escanaba, Mich., on Lake Michigan. The ore was loaded into boats for shipment to Inland's Indiana Harbor Works at East Chicago. Normally, ore can be loaded into boats at the Twin Ports, but the locks at Sault Ste. Marie had already frozen. Boats that load at Escanaba don't need to use the Soo locks, so the shipping season is longer.

The 1990 Inland move turned into an additional three-year contract. Early in 1994, Inland and WC signed a contract to move 500,000 tons of ore each winter sea-

When Wisconsin Central acquired the Fox River Valley Railroad, it gained a second main from North Fond du Lac to Oshkosh. The addition of Geneva Steel ore trains to the already growing number of regular freights on the Neenah and Black Wolf subs made both tracks necessary. On October 5, 1994, three SP C44-9Ws, led by 8112, pull a Geneva train through Van Dyne, Wis. The former FRVR main which the train is using has been redubbed the "Black Wolf Running Track." Between North Fond du Lac and Black Wolf, dispatchers can use both lines in either direction depending on traffic and congestion. — *Mike Guss*

A rainbow of motive power including SD45s 6559 and 6519 pulls a train of natural ore through Mukwonago, Wis., destined for the EJ&E at Leithton, Ill. Use of the DM&IR ore cars made these trains the heaviest for their length to ride WC rails. Even though the 100-car trains were little more than a half mile long, they weighed in at almost 9,000 tons, making them much more difficult to operate for crews used to normal-length hopper cars. On dry days such as this October 30, 1994, morning, the natural ore marked its passage with a cloud of red ore dust. — *Otto P. Dobnick*

In November 1990, Inland ore trains heading east required pushers through the Blue Hills between Cameron and Ladysmith. On November 18, WC SD45 6533 is the pusher as it leans into a curve along the Pickerel Lakes west of Weyerhaeuser, Wis. The distinctive trains of ore cars, slicing through forests and along lakes, were reminiscent of Soo Line ore trains that used similar secondary lines to move ore off of the Gogebic and Cuyuna Ranges. — *Otto P. Dobnick*

son, which translates to about 8,000 carloads. The ore was stockpiled at C&NW's Escanaba ore dock facility until the Lake Michigan shipping season opened. For this move, WC typically operated one eastbound loaded train and one westbound empty each day. Unlike the first Inland move, WC received the trains directly from the Missabe at Steelton in Duluth and delivered them to the C&NW (later to UP) at Hermansville via Ladysmith, a shorter route than through Cameron. This was made possible by WC's 1992 acquisition of the Superior lines from Soo and C&NW. Inland shipped 4,044 carloads over WC in 1994.

There have been other special iron ore moves. In September 1993, 10 trains were operated for Gulf States Steel from the Minorca mine to Gadsden, Alabama, in cooperation with DM&IR and CSX. In January and February 1994, Armco Steel contracted with WC to run eight 105-car trains from Eveleth Mine's Fairlane Plant near Forbes, Minn., to Chicago, where the trains were given to CSX for movement to Middletown, Ohio. In March 1994 Weirton Steel contracted for four trains from the Tilden mine near Palmer, Mich., to Weirton, W. Va. Also participating in this haul were C&NW and Conrail.

Other moves once again brought traditional ore jennies back onto WC rails. In October 1994, some rare shipments of natural iron ore off Minnesota's Mesabi range proved to be too sticky to flow into ore boats. WC, teaming up with EJ&E and DM&IR, came to the rescue to deliver 2,379 carloads from the Auburn Mine to waiting blast furnaces at Gary, Indiana. The trains used Missabe Road's fleet of traditional 65-ton low-side ore cars, but each road's power was used. Another 300,000 tons (more than 40 trains) of Auburn ore moved over the same route beginning in August 1995. From January to April 1995, high demand for steel kept Missabe ore cars rolling and loaded with taconite from the Minntac plant to the USX Gary Works in northwest Indiana. This time, high traffic levels on WC necessitated the use of run-through Missabe power for the trains.

THE BIGGEST CONTRACT — GENEVA STEEL

On February 9, 1994, Wisconsin Central announced its largest ore move ever when it unveiled a new agreement with Utah's Geneva Steel and Southern Pacific. The agreement called for WC and SP, together with DM&IR, to move more than 26,000 carloads of taconite yearly from the Minnesota mine more than 2,300 miles to Geneva's mill at Vineyard, Utah, south of Salt Lake City — the longest and largest all-rail iron ore move in the country. Even more remarkable is that this contract, worth at least $50 million in annual revenue, was secured from C&NW and UP which had handled Geneva ore for over ten years on a route 600 miles shorter.

The secret to successfully underbidding UP and C&NW for the contract was SP's ability to back-haul low-sulfur coal shipments. The Geneva mill opened in 1944, using iron ore and later taconite from mines in Utah and Wyoming. In 1983, then-parent USX ordered pellets to start coming from the more efficient and underutilized Minntac facility in Minnesota. The all-rail routing was DM&IR-C&NW-UP. This worked well for UP until it lost a convenient backhaul of coal to fill all those empty hopper cars heading east. Because of the location of SP's western coal mines and the location of its coal customers in the

Midwest, SP was able to take advantage of UP's lost back-haul with its own. This gave Geneva a much lower rate for moving taconite west. Thus, WC and SP were able to win the Geneva contract. Winning the Geneva business was a big victory for WC's John Carey, then Assistant Vice President–Marketing, who had helped assemble the original Geneva Steel move when he was with the C&NW. When he came to WC, one of his top goals was to capture the Geneva business for his new employer, a goal he finally achieved in 1994.

Geneva Steel has been an important new customer for Wisconsin Central. It is the only integrated steel mill operating west of the Mississippi River. With modernization programs under way in the contract's first year, the plant's annual output was expected to grow from 1.5 million tons to 1.9 million tons. Because of increased production, WC and SP were asked to start the move early. Initially, there were to be 20 trainloads a month, increasing to 30 a month by 1996. Heavy demand caused the level of traffic to increase to 29 trains a month by November 1994, and by year's end, Geneva had received 10,419 carloads via WC and SP. Eventually the trains ran daily, and in 1995 Geneva was WC's number-two customer in number of carloads.

PROSPECTS

Both the multiyear contracts and the limited-term or seasonal contracts have added significant traffic to WC lines. The 1,200 cars of iron ore handled during the first ore season had grown to 19,000 carloads in 1993, and to 32,000 carloads in 1994. Much of this traffic moves year-round, rather than only during the winter months, and the total reflects only a partial year of Geneva train movements.

The ore traffic alone has, in effect, made the Superior to Chicago route WC's main line.

There have been other additions to WC's fleet of unit trains in addition to taconite ore. WC regularly handles unit coal trains to Wisconsin Public Service plants at Green Bay and Wausau. A 1995 addition to the fleet was a contract for moving coke, a byproduct of oil refining. WC handles unit trains of coke coal, which originated on the Soo Line at Koch Refining at the Roseport industrial complex in Inver Grove Heights, Minn. The coal is destined for consignees in Green Bay and Mobile, Ala., via interchange with Illinois Central. Trains are interchanged to WC at Cardigan Jct. (north of St. Paul) and travel to Green Bay or to Chicago to hand over to the IC.

More ore traffic was on tap for WC. The Algoma Central acquisition in early 1995 added 60 carloads a day to the total. WC hosted regular ore moves from mines on the Marquette Range to the Algoma Steel mill in Sault Ste. Marie, Ont. Algoma Steel holds a 50 percent interest in the Tilden Mine on Lake Superior & Ishpeming, where the trains originate, transferring to the WC at Eagle Mills (near Marquette) for the ride across the former South Shore main through the Upper Peninsula. Prospects are also good for moves from the sintered ore mine on Algoma Central at Wawa, Ont. In 1997, WC will gain its own ore dock in Escanaba when it purchases UP's former C&NW facilities.

At start-up, Carey, who is the person most responsible for going after the iron ore business, predicted that metallic ores would one day be the number one commodity on the new railroad. At the time, not many of his colleagues took him very seriously. In 1996, the year

Only yesterday . . . The far northern reaches of today's Wisconsin Central once hosted extensive iron ore tonnage. The ore was mined underground on the Gogebic Range in the Ironwood, Mich., area and taken to Soo's massive ore dock in Ashland, Wis. On a warm, June 26, 1962, afternoon, the now dormant Bessemer branch was still very much active with Soo GP9 413 in charge of a local mine run arriving in Ironwood. The cut of ore would be taken to Hoyt Yard west of Hurley, Wis., where it would be classified into a road train. From Hoyt, trains rolled west to Mellen, then north to Ashland. The Gogebic Range was last mined in 1965; it is still rich in high-quality ore, but the ore is too deeply buried for economic mining. — *Robert C. Anderson*

Carey retired, however, it appeared as if his prophesy was coming true, with metallic ores inching up as the number two commodity on the railroad behind paper. In terms of carloads handled, U. S. Steel was WC's number one customer in 1994, shipping 40,688 units, a 35 percent increase over 1993. Clearly, as far as Wisconsin Central is concerned, the future of iron ore in the upper Midwest is on its rails.

Wisconsin Central rosters but a single SW1, stationed at North Fond du Lac to switch the shops. The locomotive was purchased from Dirk Lenthe of Fargo, N.D., who owns WC's business car *Prairie Rose*. Number 1 is switching a GP30 and an SD45 at Shops on September 18, 1993. Contrary to some reports, the unit wasn't purchased because it fit on the Shops turntable with an SD45 — although happily that turned out to be the case. Constructed in 1941 for New York Central, the veteran is still going strong in the 1990s. It was named *Francis J. Wiener* at a ceremony at Shops on September 29, 1990. Wiener was employed by the Soo for 35 years and was an active railfan who served as WC's unofficial company photographer at Shops until his death.
— *Robert C. Anderson*

7

THE HORSEPOWER STABLE

WISCONSIN CENTRAL'S MOTIVE POWER

Like most other aspects of the company, the story of Wisconsin Central's motive power fleet can be summed up in one word: growth. In 1987, after the initial fleet was on-line, WC owned or operated 85 locomotives. By 1995, after the acquisition of FV&W and ACR, the fleet had tripled to 240 units. Thanks to continuing increases in traffic, notably metallic ores, Wisconsin Central has been forced to continually add motive power and has built up a reliable fleet despite many units being over 25 years old.

Credit for the reliability of WC's locomotives belongs to the capable people at the shops in North Fond du Lac and Stevens Point. Both facilities are equipped to perform heavy overhauls. North Fond du Lac concentrates on running repairs and heavy mechanical work, while Stevens Point specializes in electrical work, including rewiring of locomotives and installation of microprocessors. In 1995 WC gained a third shop, the Algoma Central facility at Steelton Yard in Sault Ste. Marie, Ont. Steelton does

Mainstay of Wisconsin Central's fleet is the SD45. Freshly rebuilt SD45 6577, constructed as a high-nose unit for Southern Railway in 1967, shows off its fresh prime mover at Stevens Point on October 13, 1994. — *Jeff Hampton*

normal repairs, routine maintenance, and truck work. Steelton also has an indoor turntable.

The man who put together WC's diesel fleet is Vice President–Mechanical Robert F. Nadrowski, assisted by Jim Fisk, Mechanical Superintendent–Locomotives. A Milwaukee Road veteran, Nadrowski was directed to find suitable locomotives for the new company prior to WC's start-up. It would need three types of diesels: high-horse-power units for road service, lower-horsepower general-purpose units for mainline and local service; and switch engines for yard and customer switching. Nadrowski and Fisk shopped the used locomotive market and found that National Railway Equipment (NRE), a Chicago-area dealer, had 40 former Burlington Northern (BN) SD45s available at a reasonable price. Arrangements were made to buy them as part of the WC start-up; the new company would close the SD45 purchase on the same day it acquired the railroad. NRE also provided an SW900 and seven SW1200 switchers. WC acquired a variety of medium-horsepower units directly from Soo Line: 17 GP30s, 5 GP35s, and 4 SDL39s. WC also leased seven Soo GP9s with the option to buy, but chose to return them at the end of the lease in early 1988.

Nadrowski also located 11 GP35Ms at Wilson Railway Equipment in Iowa. These units had been rebuilt by their original owner, Missouri Pacific, by removing their tur-bochargers, installing 645 power assemblies, and rewiring the locomotives. They were then rerated from 2,500 horsepower to 2,000 horsepower.

When WC's start-up was delayed, NRE leased 20 of the SD45s to Southern Pacific until WC could begin operation. Several other units were leased out as well. So, when start-up finally and suddenly came, WC found itself short of power — only 46 of the planned 85 locomotives were on hand. The new company was forced to lease an assortment of motive power, including two Alcos from Green Bay & Western, the GP9s and several ex-Milwaukee GP20s from Soo Line, EMD switchers from Minnesota Commercial and Indiana Harbor Belt, and 14 GP35s from Conrail. With such a hodgepodge, many units had difficulty and trains ran late, but by early 1988 things had settled down considerably and the last of the leased units were returned.

In Wisconsin Central's early years another source of leased motive power was the Oxford Group, Inc. Oxford was formed to acquire, refurbish, sell, and lease loco-motives. Its principals included some of WC directors and officers. The initial Oxford fleet included eight SW1500s, five SDL39s, and nine SD45s of N&W and SP heritage; eventually WC acquired all the SDLs and switch-ers. In July 1988 Oxford and WC agreed that WC would provide services and materials for the Oxford fleet. Under the pact, WC refurbished the SD45s at North Fond du Lac. Occasionally WC leased locomotives, purchased parts, and even bought surplus diesel fuel from Oxford. While the SD45s rebuilt at Shops wore WC paint, Oxford is a separate corporation unrelated to WC. The SD45s were eventually sold to Wheeling & Lake Erie, and the other power elsewhere. Oxford still exists but no longer owns locomotives.

For financing purposes and to keep the rolling stock separate from the rest of the company, at start-up WC established a wholly owned subsidiary company for the locomotive and car fleets, WCL Railcars, Inc., which owns or leases WC's locomotives and freight cars. Each loco-motive is stenciled on the frame to indicate that Railcars is the owner.

Wisconsin Central's colorful diesel paint scheme has been a favorite of employees and fans almost from start-up, but its origins are surprisingly simple. The maroon and gold colors are based on the original wine red and gold used by the turn-of-the-century WC. In a 1995 interview, Nadrowski recalled how the colors came to be used. "I sketched out some ideas on how I thought the colors should be applied on a locomotive. I wanted a gold stripe that was as wide as the cab window, and ran the length of the locomotive. I put the words 'Wisconsin Central' along the stripe on the long hood along with the number. Safety striping was to be used on both ends, and the WC shield on the sides of the cab. The underbody would be black. We were at a meeting prior to start-up, and one of the consultants we were using came in with a few WC caps, done up in maroon and gold. I took the caps and my sketches and mailed them to NRE, which was painting an SD45 for us, and to Wilson, which was doing the GP35Ms, and I told them that's how I wanted them painted, and to use the colors on the caps."

The first unit to wear the colors was GP35M 4011 at Wilson. NRE took Nadrowski's suggestions to the extreme with its first repaint, SD45 6677; the safety stripes were significantly larger than on the GP35Ms and ended up looking like huge Vs. Subsequent SD45 and several other repaints included a thick V on the nose similar to the one applied to the GP35m's by Wilson. A few switchers received large V-stripes on both ends, and some later had an outline of a pine tree applied on the hood to honor the paper industry; others have a simple stripe on the hood.

For WC's first birthday, SD45 6655, since retired, received a special paint scheme: on the hood above the name was stenciled "October 11, 1988 — Our First Anniversary." The most dramatic change was a reworking of the nose stripes. The WC shield was applied to 6655 in what appears to be an upside-down version of the pine tree or "wings" that adorned maroon Soo Line F and GP noses in the 1950s and 60s. The WC design was suggested by Stevens Point car man Steve Koth. When it was first applied, the sketches of the "tree" were hard to read, and it was actually applied upside-down. As it turned out, the WC upside-down design looked good anyway, and it quickly became the standard. In an era of mundane railroad paint schemes, Wisconsin Central's has been widely hailed as one of the best in railroading.

WC's repainting program began slowly but deliberately. After early use of cheaper paints, in 1990 Dupont Imron urethane paint became the standard. While expensive, Imron lasts longer and holds up better after repeated washings — WC tries to wash its road locomotives every 45 days. Because of the sheer size of the fleet it took several years until repainted units outnumbered "heritage" ones. As a consequence, power was decked out in a variety of colors: Soo gray and red, Milwaukee Road orange and black, SP scarlet and gray, and faded BN green. Switchers were among the first units to all be repainted, followed by the SDL39s and ex-Soo GP35s. Since WC's SD45 fleet was much in demand, repainting of this group was slower. The units' appearance deteriorated as time passed, and many fans tagged them "green weenies."

One interesting story regarding locomotive painting pertains to the SDL39s. Ever hear of WC 7073? Nadrowski recalls: "We sent three of the SDL39s to Paducah, Ky., to be repainted by contractor VMV. They stripped down the units, and when it came time to paint the numbers back

Unlike many regional railroads, WC requires a large number of switch engines, owing to the many pulp and paper mills that have to be switched. Since much mill trackage is less than perfect, light switchers are well suited for the task. WC assigns switchers to yards at North Fond du Lac, Neenah, Green Bay, Gladstone, Rhinelander, Sault Ste. Marie, Ont., Stevens Point, Wisconsin Rapids, and occasionally Waukesha. In 1996, the company rostered 24 switch engines of five models. On October 1, 1989, SW1200 1236, formerly owned by Southern Pacific, is working the west end of Stevens Point yard. Note the unusual V-shaped safety stripes on the cab. — *Otto P. Dobnick*

WC originally kept track of the status of its locomotives by using a system map drawn on a metal board. Color-coded magnets, which had numbers matching each unit, were moved around the board as locomotives traveled. On March 23, 1990, chief dispatcher Pat McNamara updates the board, which was kept in the chief dispatcher's office in Stevens Point. McNamara, who had been dispatching trains since 1957, retired in March 1991 after 40 years of service with WC and Soo Line. The board was scheduled to be replaced by a computerized locomotive tracking system.— *Otto P. Dobnick*

Two rebuilt GP40s on train T220 are squeezing around the connecting track between Green Bay & Western and WC main lines at Black Creek, Wis., on December 8, 1992. WC inherited trackage rights from Soo Line over the GB&W between Green Bay and Black Creek. The "Green Bay Route" did not permit six-axle foreign road units over the trackage, so GP40s were regulars on trains out of Green Bay. With the FV&W acquisition in 1993, the restriction was eliminated. — *Steve Glischinski*

on, they looked in the cab and saw the serial number on the radio. They assumed that was the number, so they painted 7073, the radio's serial number, on the unit. I have a picture of it in my office." Naturally, after WC officials saw the "7073" the situation was quickly corrected.

Several times, WC has marked anniversaries or recognized people by naming locomotives. In addition to first anniversary unit 6655, in 1994 SD45 6520 was repainted for WC's seventh and Fox Valley & Western's first anniversary. It wears special lettering on the nose, sides, and back end. At the suggestion of Scott Ganz, a locomotive engineer at North Fond du Lac, SD45 6572 received the words "Customer Minded Employees" along its long hood. One of WC's founders, former Illinois Governor Richard B. Ogilvie, is honored by SD45 6513 (ex-6523). Ralph C. Bryant, a WC locomotive engineer who died of a heart attack, was honored by his fellow employees on October 13, 1990, when GP40 3015 was named for him. Ironically, the unit became the first WC diesel to be written off because of a wreck; it was destroyed in a head-on collision in Green Bay, Wis., on January 24, 1995. The North Fond du Lac shop switcher, SW1 number 1, was named for long-time Soo employee and village resident Francis J. Wiener, who became WC's unofficial company photographer for all locomotives and cars outshopped there prior to his death in 1990. At the request of *Model Railroader* magazine, WC applied a special MR 60th Anniversary emblem to boxcar 26173.

MORE POWER

Most of WC's ex-Soo GP30s never saw new paint, thanks to the company's first large post-start-up diesel purchase. On July 16, 1990, the WC board approved the purchase of 17 secondhand GP40s from the Gateway Western Railway. WC wanted more-reliable, higher-horse-power units, and the GP40s would fill the bill nicely. It was a happy circumstance that exactly 17 GWWR GP40s were available, enough to eventually replace the GP30s and their troublesome Alco trucks and GE traction motors, although that was not the primary reason behind the purchase. To get the GP40s up to snuff immediately, WC decided to test contract rebuilding. "We wanted to see how competitive outside shops were, and how we (WC) compared with others," Nadrowski recalled in 1995. "Plus we wanted to get all the units in service as quickly as possible, so timing dictated an outside shop be used." The Livingston (Montana) Rebuild Center (LRC) won the contract to overhaul eight of the units; WC did the remaining nine. An interesting aside is that when the units were painted at LRC, the engineer's side lettering was incorrectly applied with the numbers toward the front instead of the rear of the units.

In the fall of 1990, mechanics at Shops were busy as they strove to get the GP40s ready while still handling normal maintenance on other diesels. The GP40s began arriving in August, and crews immediately went to work restoring the 20-year-old units to like-new condition. They stripped down diesel engines, then installed new bearings, connecting rods, and power assemblies, as well as new stainless-steel piston rings. They replaced the 10-kilowatt auxiliary generators that came with the units with 18-kilowatt models that could handle all-electric cab heat, part of a general upgrading of locomotive cabs. Workers also replaced air compressors, batteries, and radiators. Trucks received rebuilt traction motors with 62:15 gearing for more pulling power and new wheels. Mechanics had to create a number of special tools to assist them in their work, including a 75-ton hydraulic ram dubbed "The Terminator," which was used to compress leaf springs. Following their overhaul at Shops, the units were painted, then shipped to Stevens Point for electrical work before being released for service. With the GP40s, WC's locomotive fleet numbered 115 units.

As the rebuilt GP40s entered service in the winter of 1990-91, the GP30s gradually went into storage. To replace their trucks and GE traction motors would require expensive modifications to the underframes. Just as it appeared as if the veterans' pulling days were finally over, a few came back to life. Traffic increases resulted in an acute shortage of motive power, and at least five GP30s were pulled from storage lines in Stevens Point and North Fond du Lac, inspected, and put back into service. If a GP30 had a major failure, it was returned to storage and another took its place. Over the ensuing three years, WC kept only the best ones running. In late 1994 and early 1995, 11 were cut up for scrap. Only three ex-Soo GP30s, 711, 713, and 715, had been repainted in WC colors, and two of those, 711 and 713, were among the five that were still in service in mid-1996. The third repaint, 715, had blown its generator and was stored, but it was donated on September 18, 1993, to the Soo Line Historical & Technical Society in a special ceremony at the North Fond du Lac shop. The Society in turn conveyed the unit to the National Railroad Museum in Green Bay.

"Ditch lights," or head-end visibility lights, would be required on all road diesel locomotives in 1997, but WC was ahead of the pack, adding them beginning in 1991. They increase the visibility of the units to motorists and pedestrians at grade crossings and enlarge the engineer's range of vision. WC's are mounted low on the pilot beam of the diesels like automobile headlights. WC is believed to be among the first to have its ditch lights begin flashing automatically whenever the locomotive horn and bell are operated by the engineer. The light control system was dubbed "Freddy's Flashers" for WC's Communication and Signal Engineer Fred M. King, who designed the circuit board and arranged to have the control units produced locally. While many railroads paid thousands for such light systems, King's design cost less than $300 each to manufacture — an example of the "We Can" attitude of WC people.

MORE SD45s

Although traffic levels on WC dipped in 1991, they rebounded in 1992 and continued upward into the mid-1990s, thanks to WC's aggressive marketing, the acquisition of three other railroads, and continued growth in taconite pellet traffic. As a result, the need for more motive power became acute. In 1992, WC came close to acquiring 23 GP39s from the Atchison, Topeka & Santa Fe Railway, but the deal fell through and the units went to Oregon's Willamette & Pacific. In April 1993, a deal was made with Santa Fe for 21 SD45s. Santa Fe is well known for its excellent diesel maintenance; it had rebuilt the vintage 1966 units in the early 1980s. The SDs were in service right up until WC bought them and were delivered in full Santa Fe lettering. Until they could be repainted, the Santa Fe markings on the cab and nose were painted over and small "WC" initials and numbers were applied on the cab sides, although the huge "Santa Fe" on the hood remained. WC added "Freddy's flashers" and snowplows to the pilots before putting them into service. All 21 were

In 1990 WC upgraded its fleet with 17 GP40s. The units, constructed for Western Pacific in 1970–1971, had last worked for another regional, the Chicago, Missouri & Western, and were conveyed to its successor, Gateway Western. WC sent eight to the Livingston Rebuild Center, a contract rebuilder operating at the old Northern Pacific shop in Livingston, Mont., while WC employees at Shops rebuilt the other nine units as seen here in fall 1990. The work included new power assemblies and radiators, and reactivating the dynamic braking.
— *Pete Briggs*

The workhorse of Wisconsin Central's fleet is the SD45. WC's initial fleet was 40 former Burlington Northern units, which included four ex-Frisco units that came to BN when it acquired that road in 1980. The BN units have been extensively reworked by WC, and almost all have been equipped with microprocessor controls that increase tractive effort. By 1995, WC had acquired a total of 107 45 series units, one of the largest fleets in operation in the United States. Two SD45s were receiving attention at Shops in June 1989. SD45 6655 has been retired and scrapped, the only SD45 removed from WC's roster. — *Stanton Hunter for Zephyr Graphics/Andover Junction Publications*

For rail enthusiasts the most photogenic locomotives in WC's horsepower stable are the six F45s and single FP45 acquired from Santa Fe in 1994 and 1995. A cowl version of the 3,600 h.p. SD45, the F45 was built only for Santa Fe, Great Northern, and Burlington Northern, while only 14 FP45s were built, nine for Santa Fe and five for Milwaukee Road. When Santa Fe ordered hundreds of new units in the early 1990s, its cowl units became surplus and WC made a deal for the seven. The company recognized the units were special and asked employees to design their own versions of WC's paint scheme to fit the unusual units. The scheme that was selected is modeled by freshly repainted F45 6651 crossing the Mississippi River in Minneapolis on February 5, 1996. — *Steve Glischinski*

repainted by the end of 1993 and renumbered 6578-6598, above ex-BN SD45s.

Why more SD45s? "They were available for the right price, and we are able to get parts for them easily," Nadrowski recalled. What about their fuel consumption, which many railroads claimed was the reason for retiring the 20-cylinder units? According to Nadrowski, it's not a problem: "Our SD45s aren't that bad on fuel. A lot of things can affect fuel consumption from railroad to railroad. We feel we do a pretty good job with the SD45s. If you would have told me eight years ago I'd have a huge fleet of SD45s, I never would have believed it. But we keep the engines tuned and are always putting newer, more fuel-efficient components on them, as well as our other power. We also emphasize fuel consumption when training engineers. Our overall fuel consumption per gross ton mile has actually been going *down* the last few years."

With more SD45s on line and the potential for more, WC renumbered the BN SD45s in mid-1993. The original sequence was simple enough: the units simply retained their previous BN numbers. This led to several number "gaps," since WC hadn't obtained all of the units in the series. Under the new plan, units were renumbered from 6495 up, filling in blank spaces. The change in numbers was due to two things: Q-Tron computer conversions and Nadrowski's desire to get the units numbered in order. "Q-Tron" is a brand of computer microprocessor equipment that improves the tonnage rating of the SD45s up to 25 percent by carefully controlling wheel slip. The equipment was gradually added to the ex-BN SD45s, and they were renumbered as they received it. WC also tested a competing system, EMD's EM2000 system, and one produced by Vapor Corporation, which it applied to several

older ex-BN SD45s. A numbering gap was kept between the former BN units, which end at 6533, and the other SD45s, since the BN's are not equipped with extended-range dynamic brakes as are other WC SD45s, but do have microprocessor controls. They are grouped together so dispatchers can readily identify them when assigning power. WC originally rated the ex-BN units at 3,200 horsepower, but as they have been tweaked by shop forces the units have been rerated to 3,450 horsepower, as are all of WC's other SD45s.

On August 28, 1993, WC's motive power fleet changed again with the acquisition of the Green Bay & Western and Fox River Valley Railroads. GB&W was among the last railroads that relied exclusively on locomotives built by the American Locomotive Company (Alco), even purchasing five used Alcos in 1979 and 1980, a decade after the builder closed its doors. WC inherited 16 of the elderly Alcos from GB&W. FRVR, like GB&W owned by Itel, was practically an all-EMD railroad. It assembled an eclectic mix of motive power during its short existence, including six Alco RSD15s from the Lake Superior & Ishpeming, but they didn't last long and were conveyed to GB&W, which never used them. FRVR began in 1988 with a motley assortment of used power from C&NW — 3 GP30s, 3 GP35s, 11 GP7s and 10 GP9s, and later added an ex-Southern SD35 and a pair of ex-BN SD24s.

WC is all-EMD, so the Alco fleet was shut down shortly after the FV&W start-up. The FRVR EMDs were kept in service, quickly restenciled with neat "WC" initials. Disposal of the Alcos soon began, but C424s 313 and 314 had one last hurrah, pulling a farewell passenger excursion across the old GB&W on October 30–31, 1993. The

Alcos were sold to short lines from Minnesota to Arkansas, and one went to a preservation group in Pennsylvania.

Twin Cities switching road Minnesota Commercial turned out to be a good customer for WC's Alcos, eventually acquiring six of them. The first three were in a December 1993 swap that sent three Alcos to Minnesota Commercial for a pair of SW1500 switchers, which WC used to replace some of the FRVR GP7s and GP9s, which were in poor shape.

In January 1994 WC again found itself in a power shortage owing to high traffic levels and an unusually harsh winter. Several of the remaining Alcos returned to service, and some were assigned to the power pool with C&NW between Iron Mountain/Antoine (Quinnesec), Mich., and Butler Yard in Milwaukee. Others were used in WC yard and local service. C&NW soon rejected the units for use on its line, and as WC's power shortage eased, the Alcos went back into storage and eventually were sold.

In spring 1994, WC purchased seven more SW1500s, this time from Norfolk Southern. Among the oldest of the model, they were built for Louisville switching road Kentucky & Indiana Terminal, which was acquired by NS predecessor Southern Railway. They lacked multiple unit capability but WC soon applied it. WC numbers its switchers by horsepower, so the MNNR and NS units went into the 1550s.

STILL MORE SD45s

In mid-1994, WC shop forces again tackled a rebuilding project, this time reworking seven high-nose ex-Southern Railway SD45s, which Nadrowski and Fisk acquired from EMD's lease fleet. WC reworked the cabs and chopped the high noses. The units arrived at Shops in June 1994 and work began on two almost immediately; the last one was completed in November. The units were numbered 6571-6577, just below the 21 Santa Fe SD45s procured the year before, and later were renumbered 6550-6556. This gave WC 180 units not counting the stored or sold Alcos. But the fleet was about to expand again.

In August and September 1994, WC acquired 31 more SD45s and two F45s from the Santa Fe. The F45s are a cowl body version of the SD45, ordered only by Santa Fe, Great Northern, and Burlington Northern. Since Santa Fe had taken out a financing agreement on 31 of the units when it rebuilt them in 1982 and 1985, AT&SF was unwilling to pay off the agreement prematurely and leased them to WC. In April 1995 the lease ended, and WC purchased the units. Two units, 6613 and 6614, had reached the end of the finance agreement in late 1994 and were immediately bought by WC and repainted.

In December 1994 two more 45-series locomotives came from Santa Fe: a single SD45 and FP45 91. The FP45, designed for passenger service and owned only by Santa Fe and Milwaukee Road, was four feet longer than the F45s to hold a steam generator for train heating. Santa Fe's nine FP45s pulled such famous trains as the *Super Chief*, and were painted in the road's beautiful red and silver "Warbonnet" scheme (developed by EMD stylist Leland A. Knickerbocker in 1937). The scheme was restored to the FP45s in 1989, and No. 91 came to the WC decked out in the famous colors, where it quickly became a favorite of employees and enthusiasts. In 1995, WC employees were asked to submit ideas to the mechanical department on how the FP45 and F45s should be repainted. The company publication included a diagram of the units, and asked employees to apply WC's colors in a

The Green Bay & Western was among the last bastions of the Alco diesel locomotive in the United States. From the time the railroad dieselized in 1950 until it was purchased by Fox Valley & Western in 1993, the road never owned a diesel from any other builder. WC and FV&W had little use for the Alcos. GB&W's fleet was shut down following the FV&W takeover, and the units shunted off to North Green Bay and Shops for storage. By early 1994 only eight of the former GB&W Alcos remained; the others had been sold to short lines. Fox River Valley also owned Alcos: six RSD15s purchased from Lake Superior & Ishpeming, which were lettered for sister Itel road GB&W after spotty use on FRVR, through none ever ran on GB&W and never operated for WC. On October 9, 1993, ex-GB&W C424 313 is switching dead Alcos into the North Green Bay roundhouse; RSD15 2404 is stored outside. An acute power shortage due to record traffic levels and a harsh winter resulted in the reactivation of at least seven ex-GB&W Alcos in January 1994. Small "WC" lettering was applied on the units' hoods. After only a few weeks in service, the Alcos were quickly stored again. In mid-1996 the last GB&W units had been sold for re-use, and all but one of the RSD15s were scrapped.
— *Otto P. Dobnick*

The SD40 and SD40-2 are among the most numerous diesel models in the United States, but WC's first came with the acquisition of the Algoma Central in 1995. ACR purchased three SD40s in 1971 (180-182) followed by six SD40-2s (183-188) in 1973. Two SD40s and one SD40-2 were wrecked on ACR prior to the WC takeover. WC renumbered the remaining six to the 6000 series and quickly modified them with FRA-shatterproof glass for service in the United States; the units are now are regulars "south of the border." Wearing a WC shield on its low nose, SD40-2 6005 (ex-187) leads a pair of GP38-2s departing Wawa, Ont., on a frigid February 2, 1995, the second day of ACRI operations. This is Algoma Central's only branch line, extending 26 miles from Hawk Jct. to Michipicoten Harbor on Lake Superior. — *Steve Glischinski*

creative manner. Over 35 replies were received, and the new scheme was an amalgamation of eight of them: a zigzag gold stripe and WC shields on the nose and sides.

The 35 Santa Fe units acquired in 1994 were numbered above the 21 that came in 1993, as 6599-6630. The cowl units got their own series, beginning at 6650. "We have good a arrangement with Santa Fe," Nadrowski recalled in 1995. "Over the years we have been able to get good locomotives at reasonable prices from them."

With all the SD45s it buys, WC has some standardized modifications that it performs. Headlights are relocated if necessary, from the nose to a position between the number boards. Units with "underslung" trucks, where the brake cylinders are down between the wheels, receive trucks with brake cylinders on top instead. The gearing is changed to a 62:15 ratio for more pulling power, and the cabs are rebuilt, including replacing hot water heating systems with electric heat. In 1995 the radios on all of WC's locomotives were equipped with earphones to reduce noise levels for operating crews and assist them with radio transmissions.

With WC's roster doubling in size, in December 1994 Mechanical Superintendent of Locomotives Jim Fisk worked out a general numbering pattern for all units except the SD45s and the SDL39s. Emulating the switchers, the system is based on horsepower. For example, ex-FRVR GP30 814, rated at 2250 horsepower, became the 2251, and 2,500 horsepower GP35 840 became 2558. The units were to be renumbered only as they came in for shop work and paint. The 3,000-horsepower, 3000-series GP40s already fit the pattern, but the 4000-series GP35Ms were scheduled to go into the 2000-series.

The horsepower-based numbering system was developed in time to incorporate Algoma Central units. When WC took over ACR on February 1, 1995, it acquired 23 diesels, including its newest: six GP38-2s, which ACR bought new in 1981. Also coming aboard were a single SW8 and an SD40, five SD40-2s, eight rebuilt GP7s and two rebuilt GP40-2s. Except for the 6000-series SD40/SD40-2s and the SW8, all the units were renumbered based on their horsepower; the SW8 became 900 instead of 800.

When Algoma Central was acquired, WC didn't waste any time bringing ACR locomotives into the fold. After the takeover, WC modified most ACR power for use in the U.S. and soon former Algoma Central units could be found in Chicago, Superior, and Minneapolis. North Fond du Lac set to work chopping the high noses of the ACR GP7s. Several WC units were sent up to Canada to replace ACR power; the only modifications needed were the placement of metal garbage cans and stretchers on the units to meet Canadian regulations.

VISITING POWER

When it can spare locomotives, Wisconsin Central has leased power to neighboring roads, such as the pre-WC Algoma Central, CN, and regional Dakota, Minnesota & Eastern. But more often than not, it's WC that is looking for more power. During the winters of 1993 and 1994, when ore movements were at their peak, WC leased six ex-Norfolk & Western high nose SD35s from EMD. The units, still painted N&W black, were nicknamed "bricks" by fans for their austere appearance.

With the advent of all-rail taconite moves, run-through power has become commonplace. Initially, WC had a pool with CSX, and it was possible to see the newest CSX GEs, as well as older power, on ore trains.

"Presidential" CSX C40-8W number 1992, which pulled President Bush's campaign special on WC, even made a special trip on an ore move. The CSX power pool was canceled in late 1993.

When the WC/Southern Pacific ore contract with Geneva Steel took effect in August 1994, SP units became commonplace on WC. As the contract commenced, the two railroads wanted to demonstrate the reliability of their service, so SP assigned brand-new General Electric C44-9s, and later new AC-traction AC4400CWs. The SP units ran through, even traveling DM&IR rails into the Minntac plant. WC balanced the pool with a dozen SD45s on SP. To reduce the number of hours owed, SP power was frequently turned at Shops Yard or Stevens Point. In 1996 another power pool was developed with Norfolk Southern, and NS units run through from Chicago to North Fond du Lac. WC power also ran through on NS.

WC power also routinely runs through on the DM&IR between Steelton and Minntac. The result is that the Missabe Road regularly "owes" horsepower hours for the time WC diesels spend on the Iron Range. To equalize hours, Missabe routinely assigns two units to WC. In the winter of 1994–1995, WC and DM&IR cooperated to move all-rail taconite and natural ore shipments from the Mesabi Range to Gary, Ind. Since WC had no power to spare, Missabe locomotives ran through all the way to the Chicago area.

In June 1995, four more Santa Fe F45s and a single SD45 arrived on the WC. With the addition of the 23 ACR units and the earlier Santa Fe SD45s, WC's fleet in mid-1996 stood at 240 units, including the ACR F units — a far cry from the 85 units of just seven years before. What about new locomotives? "With our hub and spoke operating system and the way we utilize our power, it's pretty hard to justify the cost of a new locomotive," Nadrowski says. With WC's corporate philosophy of "growing the business," it's a pretty good bet the "horsepower stable" of used locomotives will expand even more in the years to come.

East of Cameron, the original Soo route to Sault Ste. Marie traverses a lonely territory known as the Blue Hills. The rolling, tree-covered hills rise 600 feet above the surrounding plains, providing a scenic backdrop for local L066 just east of Canton on May 19, 1993, as it heads back to Ladysmith from switching duties at Barron and Rice Lake. — *Steve Glischinski*

8

TRAVELOGUE

SUBDIVIDING THE WC

At start-up, Wisconsin Central was divided into three divisions for management and operating purposes. The Eastern Division, headquartered in North Fond du Lac, encompassed all WC lines south and east of Neenah plus the Shawano Sub from Neenah north to Argonne. The Western Division, based in Stevens Point, included all lines west of Neenah and Argonne. The Michigan Division, based in Gladstone, was all lines east of Argonne (the dividing point between the Michigan and Eastern divisions was later shifted to White Lake).

In August 1993, the Eastern Division nearly doubled in size with the addition of 305 miles of ex-Fox River Valley and Green Bay & Western routes. To manage the trackage more effectively, on November 1, 1993, WC formed the Fox Valley Division. Based in Neenah, it consisted of lines from Winnebago (8 miles south of Neenah) to Dale (13 miles west of Neenah), from Neenah to White Lake, the ex-FRVR lines from Neenah to Green Bay, and eight branch lines, including the Manitowoc line and the former GB&W from Kewaunee to Scandinavia (the GB&W west of Plover was added to the Western Division). This reduced the Eastern Division to 260 miles: the Chicago-Winnebago main line and the former FRVR from Butler (Milwaukee) to North Fond du Lac and Oshkosh. The Michigan Division was unchanged. Algoma Central is managed as an independent entity with dispatchers at Steelton Yard in Sault Ste Marie, Ont.

A summary of what has happened to the other railroads in Wisconsin might be helpful. The Soo Line Railroad bought the Milwaukee Road in February 1985 and merged it January 1, 1986 — and essentially said, "I'll move into your house." In the late 1980s Soo Line's parent, CP Rail, first tried to sell Soo Line, then turned around and acquired full ownership. In the mid-1990s CP applied the name "CP Rail–Heavy Haul U. S." to the Soo Line Railroad; in 1996 CP Rail went back to its old name, Canadian Pacific Railway. Union Pacific bought and merged the Chicago & North Western in 1995.

At startup two dispatchers at Stevens Point worked the entire railroad: the east desk covered all lines east of Point and south of Lily (between White Lake and Argonne), while the west desk handled the remainder, including Upper Michigan. When the Fox Valley & Western came into the fold, a north dispatcher was added.

With traffic increases and in anticipation of Metra commuter service out of Chicago, in January 1996 WC reorganized the territories and added a fourth dispatcher. The east dispatcher now handles only the main line from Chicago to North Fond du Lac. The west desk works the main lines from Stevens Point to Minneapolis and Superior, and branch lines from Spencer to Medford and Withrow to Amery. The central dispatcher works the main line from North Fond du Lac to Stevens Point plus the ex-FRVR Black Wolf Sub through Oshkosh, the West Bend Sub from North Fond du Lac to Granville, the "Valley" line, and the ex-GB&W Whitehall Sub from Plover to East Winona. The north dispatcher handles all lines in Upper Michigan, the original Soo main line from Almena east, the Ashland and White Pine Subs, the lines out of Neenah to Green Bay, Argonne, and Manitowoc, the former Milwaukee Road from Greenleaf to Canco, near Milwaukee, and the east end of the former Green Bay & Western

In 1996 WC mileage totaled 2,817 — 1,834 miles of WC track, 466 miles owned by Fox Valley & Western Ltd., Algoma Central's 322 miles, and 195 miles of trackage rights on other railroads.

The focus of this chapter is a description of the main lines from Chicago to Superior and Minneapolis, with brief highlights of WC's secondary and branch lines. The text and photos follow the system from east to west.

CHICAGO SUBDIVISION

Stretching 147.5 miles from Forest Park, Illinois, to Shops Yard in North Fond du Lac, Wis., the Chicago Subdivision is WC's most important line. It funnels two-thirds of all freight handled by the WC into the all-important Chicago gateway. The number of trains on the line has steadily increased since start-up. By 1996 it was carrying more trains than the Soo Line ran, even in the days of scheduled passenger service. An average weekday sees 34 train movements on the subdivision, including time freights, intermodals, locals, and ore, coal, and rock trains, plus Wisconsin & Southern movements on the busiest segment of the Chicago Sub, between Duplainville and Slinger, Wis. Trains move fast across this subdivision: the general timetable speed is 50 mph.

From Forest Park north to Rugby Jct., Wis., few streets and highways parallel the line closely. The speed of the trains, the cross-country nature of the southern and middle sections of this sub, and highway traffic conditions in populated areas make following WC trains difficult at best. Nevertheless, there is a lot to see along the Chicago Sub.

WC's principal facility in the Chicago area is the former Soo Line yard at Schiller Park (near O'Hare airport, at milepost 17). Soo Line had turned the yard into an intermodal facility and abandoned the engine terminal after it acquired the Milwaukee Road and consolidated its operations at nearby Bensenville Yard, but thanks to Metra's new North Central commuter line improvements, the track layout in the area has been upgraded and improved.

Schiller Park is the base for WC locals and transfers that work the Chicago terminal. Some WC freights use a connection at B-12 to reach the Indiana Harbor Belt's Norpaul Yard, and can continue south to the west end of Belt Railway of Chicago's Clearing Yard. Freights can also use the new Metra connection to reach the BRC at Cragin and enter Clearing's east end. However, most WC freights continue south out of Schiller Park and move onto Baltimore & Ohio Chicago Terminal rails at the end of WC-owned track, milepost 10.9 at Madison Street in Forest Park (B&OCT is a CSX subsidiary). Trains destined for Illinois Central's Markham Yard or Norfolk Southern's Calumet Yard follow the B&OCT to Rockwell Street, roll through Union Pacific's giant Global One intermodal yard, then follow the St. Charles Air Line along the south side of downtown Chicago to IC's lakefront freight mainline. Trains destined for CSX's Barr Yard near Blue Island continue south on the B&OCT at Rockwell Street and use a part of the former B&O passenger route to the southside suburbs.

Just 1.5 miles south of Schiller Park is Tower B-12, where the WC main crosses the Soo Line (ex-Milwaukee Road) and Metra Milwaukee District West Line route. A new double-track connection controlled by the manned B-12 interlocking tower enables Metra commuter trains operating over WC from Antioch to travel to Union Station.

Between Tower B-12 and Antioch Metra commuter trains share the high iron with WC freights through rapidly developing Cook County and Lake County suburbs. Extensive capacity improvements were made to accommodate the commuter trains along this 35-mile stretch, including new signals and CTC, major track rehabilitation, and lengthening of several sidings. Speed limits here are 79 mph for passenger trains, 60 mph for intermodal, and 50 mph for freight. Major sidings are at Schiller Park,

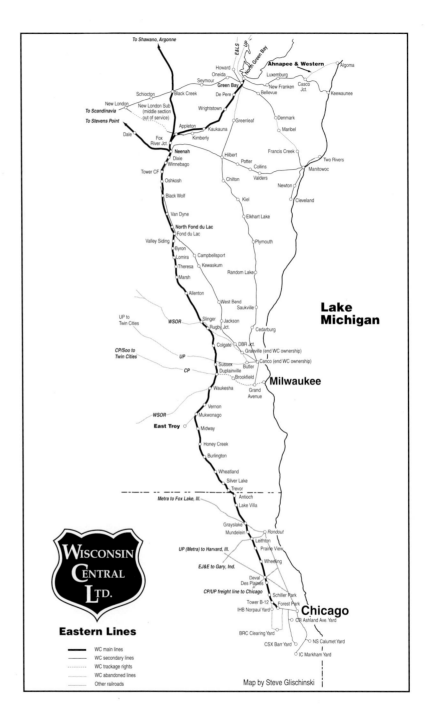

The unmistakable skyline of Chicago appears in the distance as Shops-Chicago train T040 rolls off the St. Charles Air Line, an elevated bypass owned by BNSF, IC, and UP that takes freight trains around the south side of the Loop. The train will soon be rolling down the Illinois Central main to Markham Yard on January 26, 1995. Because WC does not own its own yard in Chicago, its freights and transfers navigate the switching district's labyrinth of trackage to reach other carriers' yards. — *Brian Buchanan*

Late afternoon sun catches Shops-Barr Yard train T044 on the bridge spanning Echo Lake in Burlington, Wis., on October 19, 1994. Trailing SD45 6520 is lettered for WC's seventh and FV&W's first anniversaries. — *John Leopard*

Two different Fox Rivers meander through Wisconsin: one flows south through the southern part of the state, and the other flows north through Fond du Lac and Green Bay. On October 31, 1987, train T042 is crossing the southerly of the two in the Vernon Marsh Wildlife Area north of Mukwonago.
— *Otto P. Dobnick*

Train T042 rattles the diamonds at Duplainville, Wis., as it roars across Soo Line's former Milwaukee Road Chicago-Twin Cities main on May 12, 1994. The explosion in WC traffic since startup resulted in the regional's mainline hosting more trains than Soo at Duplainville.
— *Scott A. Hartley*

Wheeling (milepost 29), Leithton (milepost 38), and Lake Villa (milepost 51).

At Des Plaines (milepost 22.8) another interlocking tower (still manned in 1996) controls the crossing of the WC, the UP freight main from Chicago to Milwaukee, and Metra's Union Pacific Northwest commuter line. Another Metra connection, to the Metra Milwaukee District North Line, is at Grayslake (milepost 44). At Leithton iron ore and taconite trains destined from the WC to Gary, Indiana, steel mills are interchanged with the Elgin, Joliet & Eastern. About a mile north of the Antioch station is the new Metra storage yard.

At the state line the scenery changes distinctly from suburban sprawl to cottages around Silver Lake (milepost 61.1). The 5,390-foot siding here was extended to 6,300 feet as part of the Metra project. West of Silver Lake the scenery changes again to rural farmlands punctuated by small cities and towns. Between Silver Lake and Waukesha important sidings are located at Burlington (milepost 72.7), Midway (milepost 80.6), and Vernon (milepost 90.9). At Mukwonago (milepost 86.2) is the interchange with the East Troy Electric Railroad, the last true interurban railway in the United States hauling both freight and passenger traffic.

At Waukesha (milepost 97.7) WC connects with Wisconsin & Southern and a UP branch from Milwaukee. The passenger depot, constructed in 1886 of lannon stone from local quarries, still stands and serves as a base for local train and maintenance crews. Small yards are located just north of the depot and north of the city along the Fox River. Another well-used passing siding is located at milepost 100, about two miles north of the Waukesha depot.

Duplainville (milepost 102.6) is a popular train-watching spot because of the grade crossing with Soo Line's Chicago-St. Paul main line — and WC trains frequently outnumber CP moves through the interlocking. A connection installed in 1986 allows interchange between the two roads and gives WC access to Soo Line's Muskego Yard in Milwaukee.

North of Duplainville the Chicago Sub traverses the rolling topography of Wisconsin's Kettle Moraine region. At Sussex (milepost 106.6), major shipper Quad/Graphics stores its private passenger train. Continuing north the next major siding is Rugby Jct. (milepost 117.7) where Wisconsin & Southern (WSOR) tracks come into view. North of Rugby Jct. the Chicago Sub generally follows State Highway 175 or U. S. Highway 41, or is between the two, making for easy access. Five miles north of Rugby Jct. is Slinger, which in 1996 still sported a depot between the WSOR and WC mains in the shadow of the former Storck Brewery. WSOR trains regularly use trackage rights on the WC to travel between Slinger and Grand Avenue in Waukesha. Quarries at Cedar Lake, just north of Slinger, and near Sussex originate seasonal mini-unit trains of rock for WC customers in northeastern Illinois.

On the last lap into Shops Yard in North Fond du Lac passing sidings can be found at Marsh (milepost 134.3), Byron (milepost 147.1), and Valley Siding (milepost 153.3), the last only three miles south of Fond du Lac. Byron is one of the most photographed areas on the Chicago Sub, thanks to the County Highway F overpass, which sits at the crest of Byron Hill, a five-mile-long, 1.09 percent eastbound (south) grade out of Fond du Lac. Pushers out of Shops Yard were common on most freights in Soo and Lake States days, but WC normally uses helpers only on loaded ore trains. Helpers usually cut off at Byron. Most of the passing sidings between Schiller Park and Shops Yard see frequent use because of the heavy volume of trains on this subdivision, and meets between three or four freight trains are not uncommon at Byron, Waukesha, and Burlington.

NORTH FOND DU LAC (SHOPS YARD)

Shops Yard at North Fond du Lac (milepost 158.4) is possibly the busiest location on the WC. Shops Yard classifies almost all traffic to and from Chicago and inspects and services many of the ore trains. Stretched out in a north-south direction along the east side of the village of North Fond du Lac and bordered by U.S. Highway 45 and Lake Winnebago to the east, the former Soo Line yard now serves as WC's eastbound classification facility, while the former Fox River Valley yard (formerly C&NW) is for westbound classification. During the 1994–1996 rebuilding of these yards, WC added several connections between them and additional tracks. The north (westbound) end of the yard is called Shops West and is at Subway Road, named for a long-gone electric interurban railway underpass beneath the former Soo and C&NW tracks. The south (east) end of the yard is called Shops East and is at Scott Street. Shops East marks the beginning of the 62-mile West Bend Sub, the former FRVR line to UP's Butler Yard on Milwaukee's northwest side.

Sandwiched between the west side of the yard and the Village of North Fond du Lac are the shop buildings and locomotive servicing facility. The main yard office is at Lakeshore Drive, which crosses the southern portion of the yard and affords a good vantage point for photographing switching activities.

NEENAH SUB — EAST END

The 90.8-mile, CTC-equipped Neenah Subdivision main line heads north (timetable west) out of Shops Yard and turns west at Neenah to Stevens Point. From North Fond du Lac to Black Wolf (milepost 166.8), just south of Oshkosh, the Neenah Sub is paralleled just to the east by the ex-FRVR main line, which WC calls the Black Wolf running track. WC intended to remove this parallel track, but it has become an important "safety valve" relieving congestion on the main line.

At Black Wolf trains swing over to the former FRVR main through downtown Oshkosh, then return to the former Soo at Tower CF (milepost 176.7), on Oshkosh's north side. Just north of CF is Winnebago siding (milepost 178.3). At Dixie (milepost 181.6) the ex-FRVR main into Neenah connects with the WC. Most of the former FRVR track has been removed from CF through Neenah; what remains functions mainly as a switching lead in Neenah.

NEENAH TERMINAL

The Neenah-Menasha area retains the typical look of midcentury industrial America, with concentrations of industrial buildings laced by a maze of switching spurs and industrial trackage. Local crews must plan their moves carefully in Neenah's factory areas, taking into consideration switchbacks, moves through other plants, and even a drawbridge. Neenah yard has been extensively rebuilt since start-up.

SHAWANO SUB AND MICHIGAN LINES

The Shawano Sub, which connects with the Neenah Sub at Neenah, stretches 118 miles to Argonne, Wis., and

On November 28, 1992, train T008 crossed the Fox River draw-bridge on the south end of Oshkosh. — *Otto P. Dobnick*

Right: Train T020 tiptoes behind downtown Oshkosh on August 1, 1992, past the site of the former Soo Line passenger depot. — *Tom Hoffmann*

Top right: On April 17, 1992, an assortment of power idles next to the former Milwaukee Road Oakland Avenue yard office in Green Bay, which doubled as a passenger station in the waning years of passenger train operations. During WC's first years, it was typical for road power to be used for switching in Green Bay during the day before leaving on road trains in the evening. — *Jeff Hampton*

Owing to paper business, Rhinelander rated its own switch job, which also ran east or west on the Bradley Sub as needed. On December 30, 1992, the conductor of the Rhinelander switch run has the unenviable task of braving blowing snow to throw switches near the Rhinelander Paper Company mill. It's 8:30 a.m., and the switch crew's cold day has only just begun.
— *Rick Knutson*

An Escanaba-bound ore train on the Pembine Sub crosses the Menominee River near Faithorn, Mich., on February 12, 1995. The power consist includes one of three Lake Superior & Ishpeming U30Cs WC leased during the 1994–95 ore season. The Escanaba trains were loaded on the Duluth, Missabe & Iron Range, turned over to WC at Steelton, and interchanged to the Chicago & North Western at Hermansville, Mich. C&NW ore cars were used on the trains since they were the only type of car that would fit through the dumping mechanism at C&NW's Escanaba dock. — *Mike Cleary*

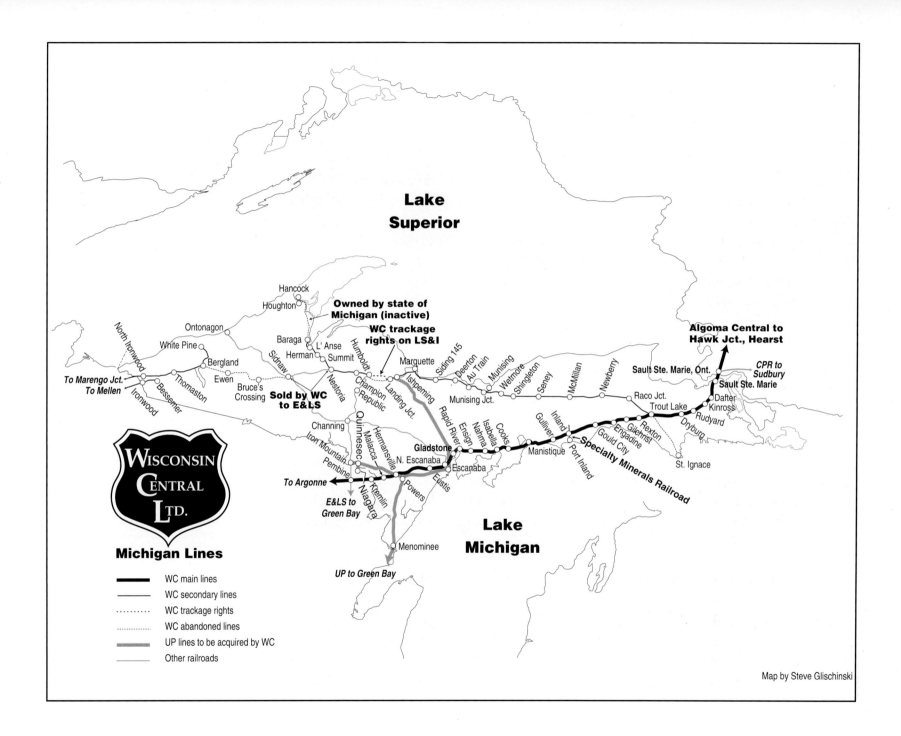

Lake
Superior

Lake
Michigan

WISCONSIN CENTRAL LTD.

Michigan Lines

— WC main lines
— WC secondary lines
······· WC trackage rights
········· WC abandoned lines
— UP lines to be acquired by WC
— Other railroads

Hancock
Houghton

Owned by state of Michigan (inactive)

WC trackage rights on LS&I

Ontonagon
White Pine
Baraga
L' Anse
Herman
Summit
Humboldt
Marquette
Siding 145
Deerton
Au Train
Munising
Wetmore
Shingleton
Seney
McMillan
Newberry

North Ironwood
Bergland
Ewen
Sidnaw
Nestoria
Champion
Republic
Landing Jct.
Ishpeming
Munising Jct.

To Marengo Jct.
To Mellen
Thomaston
Bruce's
Crossing
Sold by WC to E&LS
Ironwood
Bessemer

Channing
Iron Mountain
Quinnesec
Hermansville
Malacca
Gladstone
N. Escanaba
Escanaba
Ensign
Nahma
Isabella
Cooks
Gulliver
Manistique
Port Inland
Gould City
Engadine
Inland
Gilchrist
Rexton
Rapid River
Rexton
Specialty Minerals Railroad

Pembine
Kremlin
Niagara
Powers
Eustis

To Argonne

E&LS to Green Bay

Menominee

UP to Green Bay

Algoma Central to Hawk Jct., Hearst

CPR to Sudbury

Sault Ste. Marie, Ont.
Sault Ste. Marie
Dafter
Kinross
Rudyard
Dryburg
Raco Jct.
Trout Lake
St. Ignace

Map by Steve Glischinski

124

provides access to upper Michigan. One mile north of Neenah on the Shawano Sub is Fox River Jct., a new connection built when the Fox River Valley was acquired. It allows WC trains to proceed directly to Green Bay via the 38-mile Fox River Sub without using the ex-FRVR route through Neenah, which was rife with grade crossings and slow track.

Trains headed for the Shawano Sub and upper Michigan continue east (geographically north) to Argonne, then head east onto the Pembine Sub and into Michigan for the 100-mile trip to Gladstone, hub of WC operations in that state. East of Gladstone the 154-mile Soo Sub provides WC access to Sault Ste. Marie and connections with Algoma Central and Canadian Pacific. Along the way is the junction with the Newberry Sub, the former Duluth, South Shore & Atlantic at Trout Lake. It reaches west 123 miles to Marquette and connects there with the 68-mile L'Anse Sub to Baraga, Mich.

GREEN BAY LINES

The Shawano Sub also provides WC with access to the east end of the former Green Bay & Western, now the Black Creek Sub, at Black Creek, 20 miles north of Neenah. The Black Creek Sub extends 23 miles east to WC's facilities in Green Bay and 37 miles west to end-of-track at Scandinavia.

Green Bay has grown in importance for WC since the FRVR/GB&W acquisition in 1993. Until then the former Milwaukee Road Oakland Avenue yard, tucked away in a residential area of Green Bay, was WC's only facility in the city. WC inherited Fox River Valley's North Green Bay and GB&W's Norwood yard facilities, but immediately shut down Norwood. Oakland Avenue was converted totally to an intermodal facility, and North Green Bay became the principal yard.

WC trains out of Green Bay serve the Black Creek Sub, as well as remnants of the 34-mile ex-GB&W Kewaunee Sub. A 15-mile remnant of the former Fox River Valley Lake Shore Sub extends from Tavil Jct. in Green Bay to Denmark. The Lake Shore Sub extended 50 miles from Green Bay through Manitowoc to Cleveland, Wis., until 1996, when WC abandoned the middle section of the line from Denmark to Maribel. Until WC acquired the Fox River Valley, most Manitowoc rail traffic was routed over the Lake Shore Sub to Green Bay, then south to Chicago, but it now moves on a more direct route through Neenah.

The busiest line out of Green Bay is the ex-FRVR Fox River Sub through Kaukauna and Appleton to Fox River Junction. It connects with the important Kimberly Sub at Appleton, which has a 9-mile route along the Fox River from Kaukauna South to Appleton. Most of the paper mills served by WC are concentrated on these two lines in the Fox River Valley or in the Wisconsin River Valley between Nekoosa and Tomahawk. Fox Valley mills produce mainly "light" papers such as tissues, towels, and napkins, while mills in the Wisconsin Valley produce corrugated stock and "heavy" papers for writing and printing.

The 44-mile Manitowoc Sub runs from Neenah to Manitowoc. At Manitowoc, it connects with the south end of the ex-FRVR Lake Shore Sub, which remains in service from Maribel to Cleveland, Wis. The Plymouth Sub, the former Milwaukee Road line from Milwaukee to Green Bay, crosses the Manitowoc line at Hilbert. Its north end, from Greenleaf into Green Bay, has been removed, but trackage remains in place from Greenleaf 88 miles to

Most WC routes don't require snow-plow extras to keep the railroad open — the exception is the lines in Michigan's Upper Peninsula. Along Lake Superior's south shore, up to 280 inches — 23 feet — of snow can fall in one season. In January 1990 a snowplow extra has been called east out of Gladstone with SDL39 589 pushing plow 302 at Kinross. — *Chuck Schwesinger*

Trout Lake, Mich., was the crossing of Soo's original main line and the Duluth, South Shore & Atlantic's route from Marquette to St. Ignace. WC pulled up the inactive line from Trout Lake to St. Ignace, but the town still serves as the junction for trains operating over the old South Shore west to Marquette and Baraga. On July 20, 1993, train T035, with SDL39 586 and SD45 6539, is banging across the diamond after picking up cars from the local from Marquette, powered by SDL39 582. — *Scott A. Hartley*

Easily making the 40-mph track speed of the Soo Sub, a pair of GP30's on train T034 are kicking snow onto the former Soo depot at Rudyard, Mich., on February 18, 1990. The train has but 23 more miles to cover before pulling into Soo Yard. — *Steve Glischinski*

In 1896 and 1897 the Munising Railroad built a 38-mile line from Munising, Mich., to a connection with the C&NW at Little Lake. The railroad was purchased by Lake Superior & Ishpeming in 1900. Eighty-nine years later, only the easternmost 5.5 miles of line, isolated from the rest of the LS&I, survived to serve a Kimberly-Clark paper mill in Munising. In 1989 WC bought the branch and rehabilitated it with financial assistance from Kimberly-Clark. The K-C mill is visible in the background as GP40 3023 on L042 switches Munising in May 1991.
— *Paul A. Bergen*

Canco, on Milwaukee's north side. WC has trackage rights from Canco 8 miles to CP's Muskego yard, but seldom exercises them, preferring the route into Milwaukee from Duplainville.

NEENAH SUB — WEST END

Westbounds leaving Neenah for Stevens Point face a 1 percent grade near milepost 191, 6 miles out of the yard (milepost 186.4), then descend into rolling territory the remaining 58 miles to "Point." For most of the distance, U. S. highway 10 plays tag with the Neenah Sub; while it parallels the line nearly the entire distance and the railroad crosses it at Dale (milepost 199.4), the only areas where it is directly alongside are west of Sheridan and between Amherst Junction and Custer. The speed limit is 50 mph on this subdivision, a 10 mph increase over Soo Line days.

Three sidings are available for meets west of Neenah; the first, 6,152 feet long, is at Anton (milepost 201.0). The next point of interest is the drawbridge over the Wolf River at Gills Landing (milepost 209.9). This low bridge is normally locked in position for rail traffic, but with notification the railroad will send out personnel to open the structure for boats too high to pass under it. The next siding is just west of Gills landing at Weyauwega (milepost 213.4), site of a major derailment and fire in March 1996. Weyauwega was incorporated in 1856 and named for an Indian chief; the name means "here we rest."

The largest town between Neenah and Stevens Point is Waupaca, 7 miles west of Weyauwega. It still has a brick depot building that dates from 1907 but is no longer used. Depots of similar design remain at Marshfield, Stanley, and Ladysmith.

The main line ducks into back country, flirts briefly with U. S. 10 at Sheridan, then swings around a curve back away from the highway to the siding at Nelsons (milepost 232.4). This siding is heavily used, since it is the last point where trains can meet before reaching Stevens Point. Just to the west, at Amherst Junction, the former Green Bay & Western main line once passed over the WC. After the GB&W was acquired in 1993, WC rebuilt a connection between the two lines that had been removed in the 1960s. This allowed WC to continue to serve a shipper at Amherst Junction, while dismantling a 20-mile stretch of the GB&W main from Scandinavia to Plover that had no customers. Highway 10 crosses over the WC main just east of the GB&W overpass, offering photographers an excellent summer morning view of eastbound trains as they pop out from under the former GB&W.

From Amherst Junction to Custer (milepost 241.6) the railroad remains south of the highway. Near a rock quarry just east of Custer the tracks duck through a cut of pine trees. At the east end of Stevens Point U. S. Highway 51 passes over the tracks, then trains immediately enter the busy Stevens Point yard (milepost 249.2). The roundhouse and depot are at the west end of the yard, and between them Soo Line 4-6-2 2713 and a caboose are on display.

STEVENS POINT — HUB OF WISCONSIN CENTRAL

The operating hub for Wisconsin Central, Stevens Point is a beautiful city of 23,000 nestled in the basin of the Plover and Wisconsin Rivers. Founded in 1839 by George Stevens, the town grew from a backwoods hamlet to a bustling village when the original Wisconsin Central arrived in 1871. Soo Line maintained a large roundhouse and shop, still used by WC for locomotive repair. The former Soo Line passenger depot, a large building erected in 1917 to replace the original depot, which was destroyed by fire, houses Wisconsin Central's operating headquarters. While the outside of the building is largely unchanged, the interior has been extensively remodeled. Customer-service offices, the training center for operating personnel, and the radio shop are on the first floor, while the second houses four dispatching desks, as well as the office of the vice president and general manager.

Stevens Point yard is one of the busiest on the system, assembling traffic by blocks for WC's hub-and-spoke operating system. The yard assembles westbound blocks for East Winona, the Twin Cities, and Superior, northbound blocks for Ashland and Wausau, and eastbound blocks for Green Bay, Neenah, and Shops Yard. Point also sorts cars for Wisconsin Rapids and Wisconsin River mill traffic and puts together numerous locals.

Just east of the depot the old "P" line, the original WC's Stevens Point-Portage branch, heads south. Although most of the line was abandoned in 1945, Soo kept a portion of it south of the Stevens Point yard to connect with Green Bay & Western's Plover-Stevens Point branch; Soo had trackage rights over 2.7 miles of the GB&W branch into Plover for interchange. The P Line remnant also serves Consolidated Paper's Whiting mill. The line is now operated as part of the 19-mile Plover Subdivision, from Stevens Point to Wisconsin Rapids.

The Whitehall Sub, Green Bay & Western's main line until it was acquired in 1993, stretches 131 miles from Plover along the Trempealeau River to the BNSF interchange on the Mississippi River at East Winona, Wis. Two of the largest shippers on this line are Badger Mining Co.

at Taylor and Arcadia Furniture at Arcadia. The latter has a large intermodal facility opened in August 1995.

SUPERIOR SUB — STEVENS POINT TO JUNCTION CITY

Westbound trains leaving Stevens Point utilize the Superior Subdivision, which stretches 205 miles from Stevens Point to Superior. CTC controls the Superior Sub west of Stevens Point 59 miles to Owen, Wis. From Owen to Superior the line is unsignaled, but in 1995 WC installed dispatcher controlled power switches at Sheldon, Murray and Sauntry sidings. Plans call for all sidings eventually to be so equipped, essentially making the entire Superior Sub CTC-controlled.

Eastbound trains will usually call the Stevens Point yard as they approach Rocky Run for yarding instructions. As they depart the yard westbound trains typically call the dispatcher for the CTC signal just west of the depot, near where GB&W's Stevens Point branch once crossed the WC main.

Once out of Stevens Point, trains quickly notch up to the 40 mph limit. The tracks again parallel U. S. 10 west of Point to Rocky Run (milepost 253.4), where the short siding is often used to store cars.

West of Rocky Run the tracks curve away from U. S. 10, coming back into sight at appropriately named Junction City (milepost 260.1), the crossing of the Milwaukee Road's Valley Line and the Soo Line main, now WC's Valley and Superior Subdivisions respectively. The lines were linked by wye tracks in the northern quadrants of the crossing. WC trains between Stevens Point and Wisconsin Rapids were forced to back around the northwest connecting track until 1992, when WC built another connection in the southeast quadrant (then

In winter WC employees frequently work long, cold hours to keep the railroad moving. On February 23, 1988, the crew of local L041 picks ice out of a flangeway in Baraga, Mich. — *Mike Polsgrove*

Look what's knocking at the side door! On May 7, 1990, L2627 sneaks past a house in Chilton. The Plymouth Sub is the province of a weekday local based in Hilbert, which travels north or south along the former Milwaukee Road line as far as necessary. — *Otto P. Dobnick*

On March 29, 1991, newly rebuilt GP40s set the Stevens Point depot to rumbling as they depart with train T017 for Wausau. The building houses Wisconsin Central's operating headquarters — *Otto P. Dobnick*

Because of WC's hub-and-spoke operating scheme, "fleeting" of trains occurs frequently at North Fond du Lac and Stevens Point, with trains departing at short intervals. During WC's first years, a parade of trains would head west from Stevens Point each afternoon between 2:30 and 4:30. On June 11, 1990, the fleet is lined up for departure at Point yard: train T003 for Superior, train T005 for Minneapolis-St. Paul, and train T011 for Tomahawk; engine 1557 is working on the Point yard job.
— *Otto P. Dobnick*

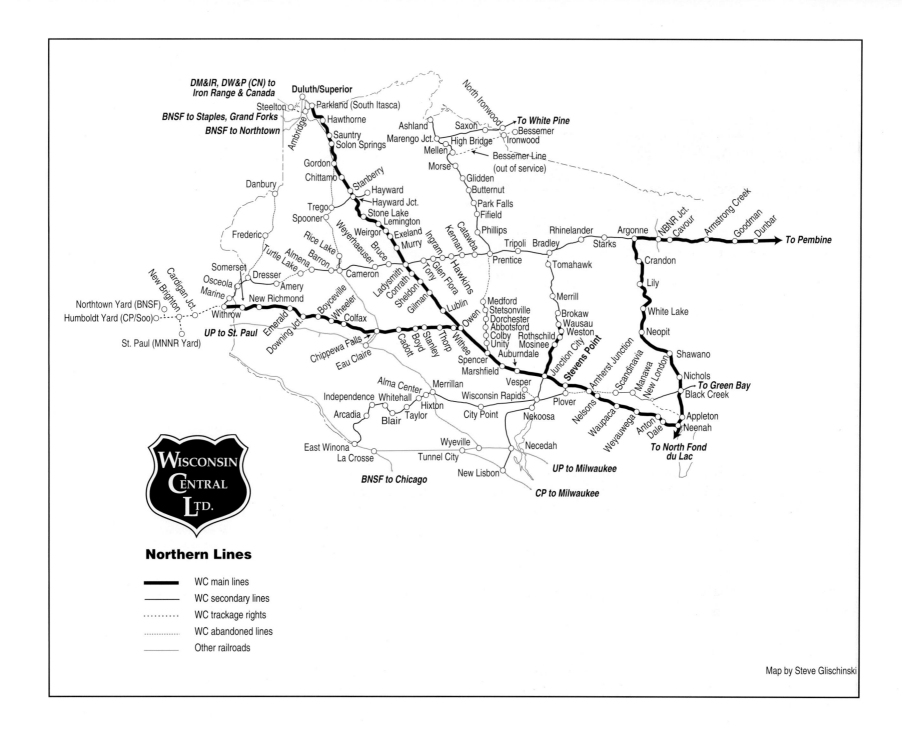

pulled up the northwest connecting track). In 1994 WC and C&NW cooperated in building a connection in the southwest quadrant to allow C&NW trains utilizing trackage rights between Superior and Necedah to change lines without backing up. C&NW (now UP) began utilizing the trackage rights on April 10, 1995.

VALLEY SUB — JUNCTION CITY TO WISCONSIN RAPIDS

The Valley Sub is one of WC's most scenic and profitable lines. WC operates daily trains over the entire line north of Nekoosa, including trains for both Wausau and Tomahawk. CP Rail's Soo Line has trackage rights on the Valley from New Lisbon to Weston for coal trains. CP and UP trains are the only operations south of Nekoosa, where there is no regular WC service.

Junction City is truly a "hot spot" on the Valley Sub. A typical day includes a pair of WC Stevens Point-Wisconsin Rapids trains (sometimes they run via Plover) a Wisconsin Rapids-Wausau turn, a Wausau-Stevens Point turn, a Stevens Point-Tomahawk turn, a Wisconsin Rapids-Neenah intermodal train, and WC or Soo Line coal trains destined for the power plant at Weston, south of Wausau. Frequently trains are forced to hold for meets at Junction City or wait for space to open up at Stevens Point.

Fourteen miles south of Junction City is Wisconsin Rapids, home of one of the two largest paper mills on WC: Consolidated Papers (the other is Mead Paper in Groos, Mich., near Escanaba). The Consolidated mill was greatly expanded in 1992, and as part of the Consolidated expansion and new road construction, WC consolidated its operations at the joint WC/C&NW Wisconsin Rapids yard, which the two roads extensively upgraded. To reach the yard more efficiently, WC also relocated the ex-Milwaukee track through the city near the Consolidated facilities. The old GB&W main, now the Whitehall Subdivision, stretches 116 miles from Wisconsin Rapids to East Winona.

SUPERIOR SUB — JUNCTION CITY TO OWEN

From Junction City through Milladore to Auburndale (milepost 272.3) the Superior Sub and Highway 10 are right alongside each other, offering the opportunity to watch burly SD45s and F45s hustle freight right outside your car window. Highway 10 crosses over the top of the main line at the west end of Auburndale and is a favorite spot for photographers. Auburndale's 6,170-foot siding is a busy meeting point. The tracks head cross-country while the highway loops away into Marshfield.

After passing a talking hotbox detector at Hewitt (milepost 277) trains enter Marshfield (milepost 280.9). This city once was served not only by WC, but by the Merrillan-Wausau line of the Omaha Road (C&NW). Soo and C&NW shared a branch from Marshfield to Wisconsin Rapids, also now abandoned. The Marshfield sidings are often used as a marshaling or storage point for WC ore trains. The large brick WC depot still stands, although it is no longer used.

West of Marshfield highway 10 parallels the Superior Sub for eight miles into Spencer (milepost 289.4), where the Medford Subdivision leaves the main, reaching north 26 miles to the town of the same name. In Soo days this was part of the Spencer-Prentice-Ashland main line. In June 1987, the Lake States Division of the Soo began using the Valley Line for Ashland-bound trains, and the line from Medford to Prentice was abandoned, although the rail wasn't until removed until 1991. North of Prentice, the 89-mile Ashland Sub remains an important

Swinging around the northeast wye connection at Junction City, a GP35/SDL39 duo creeps by one of Wisconsin's ubiquitous local taverns en route to Wausau on May 13, 1990. — *Otto P. Dobnick*

The corporate emblem of the Employers Insurance Company of Wausau combines the former Milwaukee Road depot with a view of the Wausau skyline as seen from the former C&NW depot. Several of the company's television commercials have featured the emblem. Train T018 rolls past the building and down the Valley Line on July 11, 1991. — *John Leopard*

The largest paper mill on the WC is the Consolidated Papers facility in Wisconsin Rapids. In September 1991, the Consolidated mill looms in the background as SW1200 1231 pauses between switching chores at the Wisconsin Rapids yard. — *Steve Glischinski*

Weyerhaeuser Corporation is one of WC's biggest shippers, and maintains one of its largest mills along the Valley line at Rothschild. The mill maintains its own locomotive to switch the complex; WC trains simply pick up and set out. In March 1991 train L018 is makes its way past the huge facility. — *Otto P. Dobnick*

From its source near the Michigan border, the Wisconsin River winds 340 miles through Wisconsin to the Mississippi River at Prairie du Chien, making it the state's longest river. Along WC's Valley Sub, the river is seldom far away, and in some areas is right along the tracks. One such place is Mosinee, where GP40 3022 is easing to a stop just north of the Mosinee Paper Corp. mill on September 26, 1991. — *Steve Glischinski*

part of the WC system, serving the Lake Superior port city of the same name, and connecting with the 77-mile ex-DSS&A White Pine Sub at Marengo Jct., Wis. The Medford Sub is now a branch, but several shippers, have kept the line viable under WC control.

SUPERIOR SUB — OWEN TO SUPERIOR

From Spencer to Owen, back roads follow the WC main line. Owen (milepost 308.5) is the junction with the Minneapolis Sub and another important meeting point for trains. It was once an important rail center. In addition to the original WC, the town hosted a short line, the Fairchild & Northeastern, and two logging lines: the Owen & Northern and the John S. Owen Lumber Co. Originally, the town was on a due east-west line of the WC from Abbotsford. When the line from Owen to Ladysmith and Superior was completed in 1908, the main line ran via Abbotsford. This was replaced in 1910 by the more direct, 19.9-mile Spencer-Owen Cutoff. The line from Abbotsford to Owen was abandoned between 1934 and 1938. However, the Owen depot was built on the original alignment and remains in 1996 at an odd angle to the "new" main line.

In Soo Line days the Minneapolis route was considered the main line, but WC's line from Owen to Superior has seen an explosion of traffic since 1989, when the first contracts were signed to move taconite pellets from the Twin Ports to Chicago. Steady growth in ore combined with increased local business and Canadian traffic from Canadian National's Duluth, Winnipeg & Pacific have helped make the Superior Sub far busier than in Soo Line days, and it is considered the main line today.

Movements on the Superior Sub are controlled by radio-issued track warrants. Following the line from Owen to Superior can be difficult, since there are few paralleling roads, and the tracks take a more direct route than the roads. Trains heading west out of Owen travel through rather uninspiring scenery through Lublin (milepost 320.4) and Gilman (milepost 328.2) to Sheldon (milepost 340.3), where just south of town the tracks cross the Jump River on an open bridge. The power switches at Sheldon are frequently utilized for meets; from there it's a quick 13-mile run to Ladysmith (milepost 353.3).

Ladysmith, on the Flambeau River, was at the crossing of Soo's Minneapolis-Sault Ste. Marie line and the original WC route to Superior. After the WC start-up, the Superior line saw renewed importance, but for a while the line east of Ladysmith to Prentice was bereft of trains. When ore trains began running from Superior to Escanaba in 1990 and the Flambeau mine opened in 1993, WC reopened the line from Ladysmith to Prentice. The east-west line is now the Bradley Sub, stretching 161 miles from Argonne through Rhinelander, Prentice, and Ladysmith to end-of-track at the tiny town of Almena, Wis. In late 1994, the diamond at the crossing of the Superior and Bradley Subs and the old freighthouse were removed and WC built a new connection behind the old passenger depot to allow ore trains to head onto the Bradley Sub without backing up. WC maintains a one-stall metal engine shed to house the local engine, which switches the Flambeau Mine south of town as well as working west to Almena, and the six-mile former C&NW Cameron — Rice Lake Sub.

The city of Ladysmith has been skillful in preserving its rail heritage. On display along the Superior Sub is Soo Line 2-8-2 No. 1011, while west of the depot on the Bradley Sub are FP7 500A and three Soo Line passenger cars, creating an image of a Soo Line passenger local of the 1950s.

The Rice Lake Sub has an interesting history. Both Chicago & North Western and Soo Line once served Rice Lake; Soo had a 6.7-mile branch from Cameron on the east-west Sault Ste. Marie route, while the C&NW line was part of the Eau Claire-Superior line. The lines crossed three miles south of town, and the interlocking was guarded by a brick tower — which still survived in 1996, among the last in Wisconsin. During WC's first four years, it used the old Soo branch to serve Rice Lake, but after it bought North Western's Cameron Line in 1992, a new connection allowed the Soo branch to be pulled up.

Northwest of Ladysmith more trees dot the landscape. After crossing the Chippewa River the tracks enter Murry (milepost 363.7), which has one of the longest sidings on the line, over 7,000 feet. West of Murry between Exeland and Weirgor State Route 48 parallels the line before it ducks into the woods. Both Weirgor (milepost 370.9) and Lemington (milepost 377.1) have pulpwood-loading sidings.

The railroad returns to civilization at Stone Lake (milepost 389.4), headquarters for a WC maintenance crew. The crew called an old Soo Line depot home until 1995, when WC built a new structure and the depot was removed. Highway 70 passes over the tracks in the middle of town and the tracks skirt the lake before swinging due north toward Hayward Junction (milepost 400.5), a new station, created in 1992 when WC acquired C&NW's Cameron-Superior route. With the sale, C&NW's 18.7-mile Trego-Hayward branch was isolated from the rest of the system, so C&NW built the connection using WC trackage rights from Superior to reach the branch. The

isolated line was sold to WC in 1996, a year after Union Pacific completed its purchase of the C&NW.

About a mile north of Hayward Junction, the Superior Sub bridges U. S. Highway 63 and enters Stanberry, another busy pulpwood loading site. The tracks cross a large marsh, then enter Chittamo (milepost 412.6) which has a 4,132-foot siding. At Gordon (milepost 420.9) westbound trains transfer off the former Soo Line and onto the ex-C&NW via a connection built in 1992. Soo and C&NW once paralleled each other through Gordon, and a bit of the former C&NW remains, dubbed Spur 422 for its milepost. Meets sometimes take place using the spur, although trains must back in or out.

From Gordon, the rails follow the St. Croix River to Solon Springs, where WC parallels U. S. Highway 53 through town. The old C&NW depot has been moved to the west side of the highway in Solon Springs for use as a restaurant. The tracks pass along the edge of Lucius Woods County Park north of Solon Springs to the frequently used siding at Sauntry (milepost 430.5). From Sauntry the tracks pass under highway 53 and swing close to the now-abandoned Soo roadbed.

Hawthorne (milepost 439.8) is the top of the 12-mile-long 1 percent grade down the South Range into Superior. Helpers on southbound ore trains usually cut off there. At the bottom of the grade is a small WC yard office at Parkland (milepost 453.7); most crews swing off their trains there. Some freights continue 6.6 miles to Duluth, Winnipeg & Pacific's Pokegama Yard, utilizing trackage rights over DM&IR from South Itasca, about a mile west of Parkland.

Empty ore trains head west (timetable north) another 6.8 miles beyond Pokegama to Missabe Road's Steelton

WC's Bradley Sub, extending 161 miles from Argonne to Almena, is one of WC's more diverse, in terms of trains. Most of the route is covered by locals, but it also hosts Wausau-Mellen through trains, which utilize a connection with Tomahawk Railway at Bradley and run to Prentice, then onto the Ashland Sub. In winter, all-rail ore trains use the route as well. On February 25, 1988, local L015 is about to pass under the U. S. 8 overpass east of Prentice.
— *Mike Polsgrove*

On February 1, 1995, an eastbound ore train bound for U. S. Steel's Fairfield Works near Birmingham, Ala., charges by the old Soo depot at Stone Lake on the Superior Sub.
— *John Leopard*

Helpers still must be used on loaded ore trains on WC's ex-C&NW route out of the Twin Ports, since it includes a 12-mile, 1 percent grade up the South Range south of Superior. Empties have an easier time of it, as this empty ore train demonstrates heading down the grade at Hawthorne on March 27, 1993. Superior-Stevens Point local L064, heavy with pulpwood gons, waits to head east. — *Otto P. Dobnick*

On the last lap into DM&IR's Steelton yard on March 27, 1993, an empty train crosses into Minnesota on Missabe's Oliver Bridge. The 2,189-foot structure was authorized on February 20, 1908, by an Act of Congress which mandated that it have two levels. The upper one is used for trains and the lower by automobiles. The bridge was built to accommodate two tracks, but the second was never constructed. — *Otto P. Dobnick*

Yard, 13.4 miles from Parkland in Gary and New Duluth, Minn. WC requested the rights into Steelton when it applied to the ICC to purchase the Cameron Line from C&NW. Access to the sidings at Steelton, which can easily handle long ore trains, was necessary since the trains often have lengthy waits to fit into their designated "loading slot" at Mesabi Range taconite plants. Depending on time and crew availability, transfer crews working out of Parkland may handle these trains. The stretch of DM&IR trackage from South Itasca to Steelton is very busy with WC, BNSF, DM&IR, DW&P, and UP trains.

Typically a WC transfer crew travels the Superior area handling interchange with BNSF, Soo Line, DW&P (CN), and Union Pacific. The UP interchange is at the latter's South Itasca Yard, about a mile and half north of the WC facility. Connections with Soo Line are handled at their Stinson Yard. To reach this yard, trains use a 3-mile stretch of WC-owned track from Ambridge (four miles west of South Itasca on the DM&IR) to Stinson. This trackage is an "absolute block" verbally controlled by the WC dispatcher and is equipped with automatic block signals.

MINNEAPOLIS SUB — OWEN TO CHIPPEWA FALLS

While the Superior Sub sees the bulk of the trains, WC's 124-mile Minneapolis Sub has become steadily busier since 1987. The route is controlled by track warrants from Owen to Withrow, Minn., where trains enter Soo Line's CTC-equipped Paynesville Subdivison, over which WC has trackage rights into Minneapolis.

From the connection with the Superior Sub at Owen, trains swing west under an old wood overpass toward the tiny community of Withee (milepost 310.5). County Road X parallels the tracks about a half mile south through

Thorp (milepost 320.5) and into Stanley (milepost 327.2), where a stone depot, now derelict, stands in the heart of town. Stanley is usually as far east as the local out of Chippewa Falls travels. County X turns south at Stanley, but State Highway 29 remains within a half mile of the tracks into Boyd (milepost 332.6), summit of a steep grade from Cadott (milepost 338.7). The grade can tax heavy trains, particularly Green Bay- and Weston-bound coal trains, which usually rate four SD45s. West of Cadott, County X again moves close to the tracks, and the tracks and the highway are practically on top of one another crossing Lake Wissota on a long fill. County J follows the tracks into Chippewa Falls, where WC rails cross UP's ex-C&NW line from Eau Claire to Cameron (the line north of Cameron was purchased by WC). After crossing the UP, the Minneapolis Sub crosses the Chippewa River on a steel bridge.

Chippewa Falls is the home of the famous Jacob Leinenkugel brewery, established in 1867 and Chippewa Falls' oldest industry. The town was an important division point for the Soo Line, but under WC control was downgraded. CF Yard (earlier called Irvine Yard) was a crew-change point for Soo, with a yard and six-stall roundhouse (which still stands in 1996, although not connected to active rails); there was also an 8-mile branch south to Eau Claire, now abandoned. When WC took over, crews simply ran through CF, but a local job was assigned to work the yard, local industries and the main line between New Richmond and Owen. WC through freights usually stop at CF yard to set out or pick up cars.

MINNEAPOLIS SUB — CHIPPEWA FALLS TO WITHROW

The Minneapolis Sub heads west out of Chippewa Falls, then swings north, passing under county highway N near Howard (milepost 358.8), a siding frequently used for car storage. County N follows the tracks to Colfax. This is scenic, rolling hill country, and the tracks alternately ride large fills and traverse cuts. At Albertville (milepost 362) an old wood bridge crosses over one of these cuts before the tracks make another swing to the north and into Colfax (milepost 369). A brick depot remains on the north side of the tracks, while an old wood freight house, converted to a residence, can be found on the south side of the tracks. The tracks cross the Red Cedar River in the woods west of town, while State Highway 170 follows to the north, then parallels the tracks into Wheeler (milepost 379.4) and on to Boyceville (milepost 386.2). Trains sometimes briefly pause in Boyceville so crews can grab a snack at establishments along Main Street. Three miles west of Boyceville is the long siding at Downing Junction, at 6,322 feet the longest on the Minneapolis Sub and a frequent location for meets.

The original Soo Line route west of Downing Jct. passed through Glenwood City to Cylon, but this was superseded in 1910 by the Roddis Cutoff, which swings north through Emerald (milepost 399.3) to Cylon (milepost 404.4). The original line was used mainly by passenger trains and local freights into the 1930s until the line west of Glenwood City was abandoned.

West of Cylon the WC swings through several curves, then enters New Richmond (milepost 413.5). Another stone depot, similar to the one at Colfax, sits south of the tracks. Just west of the depot the old Omaha Road line from Hudson to Spooner, Wis., once crossed the WC, but New Richmond is a one-railroad town now. West of town the WC right-of-way follows the New Richmond Cutoff. After the original Wisconsin Central was completed to the Twin Cities in 1884, the company undertook a series of line relocations and improvements that continued after Soo Line leased the railroad. Among these was the 18-mile New Richmond Cutoff between Withrow, Minn., and New Richmond, opened in 1911. The project included a new bridge over the St. Croix River (at milepost 424.3) and a major line relocation that reduced grades from 1.3 percent to 0.5 percent. Curvature was reduced from a maximum of 6 degrees to slightly over 1 degree.

When Soo decided to build a new bridge across the St. Croix River near Somerset, it originally considered a concrete arch bridge because of the permanent nature of such structures. The idea was quickly dismissed because the weight of the spans would have increased the cost of foundations, and the necessity of winter construction prevented the use of concrete. Steel was used instead for the five-arch bridge, which was completed in 1911. Now a National Engineering Landmark, the bridge was named in 1992 for the late WC Chairman Donald J. McLachlan. It is one of two WC crossings of the St. Croix; the other is south of Osceola on the Dresser Sub.

From the bridge trains need travel only seven miles to reach the tiny community of Withrow (milepost 432.1), junction with the 39-mile Dresser Sub and the end of WC-owned trackage. Freight service on the Dresser Sub is provided with WC equipment manned by members of the nonprofit Minnesota Transportation Museum, which also runs seasonal excursion trains over the route under the name Osceola & St. Croix Valley Railway. Passenger trains operate during the summer months out of the restored Soo Line depot at Osceola. Soo Line also has trackage rights between Withrow and Dresser to reach a trap-rock quarry.

On September 8, 1992 train T006, en route from Minneapolis to Stevens Point, rides one of the fills on the New Richmond Cutoff east of Somerset. The cutoff was part of a 1911 line relocation in conjunction with the building of the new bridge across the St. Croix River. — *Steve Glischinski*

Train T205, a new Stevens Point-St. Paul service begun only a month earlier, is observing the 25 mph speed limit of the St. Croix River high bridge as it heads into Minnesota on October 13, 1994. — *Steve Glischinski*

Minnesota Commercial and Twin Cities & Western locomotives wait as WC train T205 arrives at its destination, the Minnesota Commercial yard in St. Paul on September 21, 1994. Stevens Point-St. Paul trains 205 and 206 were inaugurated September 14, 1994. — *Steve Glischinski*

Wisconsin Central interchanges with BNSF in Minneapolis at BNSF's huge Northtown Yard, reached via trackage rights over the Soo. On July 17, 1994, the Minneapolis skyline is visible in the distance as a WC transfer eases into Northtown at 7 a.m. — *Steve Glischinski*

On February 2, 1991, SD45's 6523 and 6531 are running late as they begin the assault on Soo's Short Line Hill en route back to New Brighton. — *Rick Knutson*

Sunset near Junction City, January 18, 1993. — *Dan Munson*

TWIN CITIES TERMINAL

From Withrow into the Twin Cities, WC relies on trackage rights over Soo Line. Soo retained ownership to ensure that WC cannot handle bridge traffic through the Twin Cities, as stipulated in the original WC purchase agreement. At Withrow, trains enter CTC territory (installed in December 1984) under the control of CP dispatchers in Minneapolis.

WC's primary terminal in the Twin Cities is in the St. Paul suburb of New Brighton, where Soo crosses the Minnesota Commercial Railway (MNNR), a terminal carrier that reaches south to St. Paul's Midway industrial district. WC uses MNNR's New Brighton yard for switching, and runs transfers from New Brighton to BNSF's Northtown Yard and Soo's Humboldt Yard in Minneapolis. WC has trackage rights on MNNR into St. Paul.

At start-up, WC served the Twin Cities with a single pair of trains between Stevens Point and Minneapolis, T005 and T006. On arrival at New Brighton, 5's power was broken up. The road crew took cars for Burlington Northern to BN's Northtown Yard in Minneapolis and tied up for the night, while a transfer crew ran to Soo's ex-Milwaukee Road yard in St. Paul. Reaching the latter involved operating over slow track on the Minnesota Commercial to St. Paul, negotiating busy terminal trackage, and climbing steep Short Line Hill west of downtown St. Paul, resulting in significant delays. On March 4, 1991, the primary Soo interchange was switched to Soo's Humboldt Yard in Minneapolis, eliminating the long, slow run into St. Paul. WC trains continue to run into the MNNR yard in St. Paul to handle interchange traffic for Minnesota Commercial, Twin Cities & Western, and UP, and intermodal traffic interchanged to BNSF's Midway Hub Center in St. Paul by Minnesota Commercial. In 1996 the "end" of WC's main line operations remained Soo's Humboldt Yard in Minneapolis — the westernmost point reached by WC trains.

ALL-TIME WISCONSIN CENTRAL LOCOMOTIVE ROSTER
August 1996

All Locomotives built by Electro-Motive Division of General Motors, except as noted

SW1 — 600 Horsepower

WC No.	Former No.	Builder No.	Date	Notes
1	CR 8480	1265	6/41	Ex-PC 8480, NYC 8480, NYC 683, nee NYC 633, named "Francis J. Wiener"

Alco RS-20 — 2000 Horsepower

WC No.	Former No.	Builder No.	Date	Notes
305	GB&W 305	78856	5/51	Rebuilt to RS-20 6/73; to Badger Mining Co., 1994; to Gopher State RR Museum
306	GB&W 306	78857	5/51	Rebuilt to RS-20 2/76; to CALM, 1994
307	GB&W 307	81286	6/55	Rebuilt to RS-20 1/75; to MNNR 307, 11/18/94
308	GB&W 308	81287	6/55	Rebuilt to RS-20 4/74; to KB&S, 1995

RS-20s are RS-3s rebuilt by GB&W Norwood Shops with 251-C engines.

Alco RS-11 — 2000 Horsepower

WC No.	Former No.	Builder No.	Date	Notes
309	GB&W 309	81931	8/56	Ex-KGB&W 309, rebuilt to 2000 hp and nose chopped 1964; to KB&S, 1995.

Alco C-424 — 2400 Horsepower

WC No.	Former No.	Builder No.	Date	Notes
311	GB&W 311	84559	9/63	To MNNR 311, 4/94
312	GB&W 312	3375-01	7/64	To IHRC, 5/94
313	GB&W 313	3382-04	1/65	To MNNR 313, 12/93
314	GB&W 314	3382-08	9/65	Ex-KGB&W 314; to MNNR 314, 12/93
319	GB&W 319	84558	9/63	Ex-CR 2474, PC 2474, nee PRR 2415; rebuilt GE Hornell 2/80; to CALM 6/94
320	GB&W 320	84553	6/63	Ex-CR 2486, nee EL 2412; rebuilt GE Hornell 3/80; to CALM 1994
321	GB&W 321	84557	6/63	Ex-CR 2489, nee EL 2415; rebuilt GE Hornell 3/80; to CALM 6/94
322	GB&W 322	84733	10/63	Ex-CR 2493, nee RDG 5204; rebuilt GE Hornell 3/80; to RT&HS, 6/94

Alco RS-27 — 2400 Horsepower

WC No.	Former No.	Builder No.	Date	Notes
316	GB&W 316	83604	3/62	Ex-C&NW 903; to MNNR 316, 1994
318	GB&W 318	83602	3/62	Ex-PNC 901, nee C&NW 901; to MNNR 318, 1993

Alco C-420 — 2000 Horsepower

WC No.	Former No.	Builder No.	Date	Notes
323	GB&W 323	3463-1	2/66	Ex-CR 2475, nee L&HR 27; rebuilt GE Hornell 12/79; to IAIS 850, 1993

SDL39 — 2300 Horsepower

WC No.	Former No.	Builder No.	Date	Notes
582	Soo 582	34273	3/69	Ex-MILW 582
583	Soo 583	34274	3/69	Ex-MILW 583
584	Soo 584	34275	4/69	Ex-MILW 584
585	Soo 585	34276	4/69	Ex-MILW 585
586	HLCX 586	7345-1	11/72	Ex-Soo 586, nee MILW 586
587	HLCX 587	7345-2	11/72	Ex-Soo 587, nee MILW 587
588	HLCX 588	7345-3	11/72	Ex-Soo 588, nee MILW 588
589	HLCX 589	7345-4	11/72	Ex-Soo 589, nee MILW 589
590	HLCX 590	7345-5	11/72	Ex-Soo 590, nee MILW 590

GP30 — 2250 Horsepower

WC No.	Former No.	Builder No.	Date	Notes
700	Soo 700	28342	3/63	Alco trucks
703	Soo 703	28323	3/63	Alco trucks
704	Soo 704	28324	3/63	Alco trucks, scrapped 1994
706	Soo 706	28326	4/63	Alco trucks, scrapped 1/95
707	Soo 707	28327	4/63	Alco trucks, scrapped 1994
708	Soo 708	28328	4/63	Alco trucks, scrapped 1/95
709	Soo 709	28329	4/63	Alco trucks, scrapped 1/95
710	Soo 710	28330	4/63	Alco trucks, scrapped 1994
711	Soo 711	28331	4/63	Alco trucks
712	Soo 712	28332	5/63	Alco trucks, scrapped 1994
713	Soo 713	28333	5/63	Alco trucks
715	Soo 715	28335	5/63	Alco trucks, donated to SLH&TS, 9/93; donated to National Railroad Museum, Green Bay for display
716	Soo 716	28336	5/63	Alco trucks, scrapped 1/95
717	Soo 717	28337	5/63	Alco trucks, scrapped 1994
718	Soo 718	28338	6/63	Alco trucks, scrapped 1994
719	Soo 719	28339	6/63	Alco trucks
721	Soo 721	28341	6/63	Alco trucks, scrapped 1994
2251	WC 814	28308	4/63	Ex-FRVR 814, nee C&NW 814
2252	WC 815	28309	4/63	Ex-FRVR 815, nee C&NW 815
2253	WC 840	28314	4/63	Ex-FRVR 840, nee C&NW 820

SW8 — 800 Horsepower

WC No.	Former No.	Builder No.	Date	Notes
900	ACR 140	A297 (GMD)	12/51	

SW9 — 1200 Horsepower

WC No.	Former No.	Builder No.	Date	Notes
1231	HB&T 31	15129	8/51	

SW1200 — 1200 Horsepower

WC No.	Former No.	Builder No.	Date	Notes
1230	MP 1107	27875	1/63	Sold to Charter Manufacturing, Saukville, Wis., 1992
1232	WC 1278	31236	2/66	Ex-MP 1278
1233	HB&T 33	31683	4/66	
1234	HB&T 34	31684	4/66	
1235	SSW 2260	29636	1/65	Ex-SSW 1072
1236	SP 2287	30254	11/65	Ex-SP 1622
1237	SP 2288	30255	11/65	Ex-SP 1623

GP7Lm — 1500 Horsepower

WC No.	Former No.	First Builder No.	Date	Second Builder No.	Date	Notes
1501	ACR 100	A262 (GMD)	8/51	A3541	6/78	Ex-ACR 155, rebuilt by GMD to GP7Lm
1502	ACR 101	A263 (GMD)	8/51	A3542	6/78	Ex-ACR 156, rebuilt by GMD to GP7Lm, nose chopped by WC, 5/95
1503	ACR 103	A272 (GMD)	1/52	A3544	5/78	Ex-ACR 165, rebuilt by GMD to GP7Lm
1504	ACR 104	A441 (GMD)	12/52	A3545	5/78	Ex-ACR 169, rebuilt by GMD to GP7Lm

1501-1504 were thoroughly rebuilt by GMD at London, Ont., and outshopped in May and June 1978 with new builder numbers. During the rebuilding components were scrambled so a unit-for-unit match may not be accurate. WC plans to chop the high noses of its ex-ACR GP7Lms.

GP7 — 1500 Horsepower

WC No.	Former No.	Builder No.	Date	Notes
1505	ACR 157	A264	9/51	Rebuilt by CN Transcona Shops 1978
1506	ACR 158	A265	10/51	Rebuilt by CN Transcona Shops 1978, nose chopped by WC, 5/95
1507	ACR 167	A274	2/52	Rebuilt by CN Transcona Shops 1978
1508	ACR 170	A442	12/52	Rebuilt by CN Transcona Shops 1978

WC plans to chop the high noses of its ex-ACR GP7s.

SW1500 — 1500 Horsepower

WC No.	Former No.	Builder No.	Date	Notes
1550	SSW 2487	33618	1/68	
1551	SP 2505	33992	7/68	
—	SP 2529	35222	7/69	Was to be 1552, number never applied, scrapped at Stevens Point
1552	MNNR 303	34724	4/69	Ex-MT 303, traded 12/93 for GB&W 313, 314, 318

1553	SP 2578	35814	4/70	
1554	SP 2594	4608-4	10/71	
1555	SP 2640	4608-50	5/72	
1556	SP 2652	4608-62	7/72	
1557	SP 2665	4608-75	7/72	
1558	MNNR 304	34725	4/69	Ex-MT 304, traded 12/93 for GB&W 313, 314, 318
1559	NS 68	31591	7/66	Ex-Sou 68, nee K&IT 68, second SW1500 built
1560	NS 70	33769	2/68	Ex-Sou 70, nee K&IT 70
1561	NS 71	33770	2/68	Ex-Sou 71, nee K&IT 71; wrecked at Green Bay 1/24/95, returned to service
1562	NS 72	33861	3/71	Ex-Sou 72, nee K&IT 72
1563	NS 73	33862	3/71	Ex-Sou 73, nee K&IT 73
1564	NS 75	33864	3/71	Ex-Sou 75, nee K&IT 75
1565	NS 76	33865	3/71	Ex-Sou 76, nee K&IT 76

GP38-2 — 2000 Horsepower

WC No.	Former No.	Builder No.	Date	Notes
2001	ACR 200	A4067 (GMD)	1981	Rebuilt by ACR 3/91
2002	ACR 201	A4068 (GMD)	1981	Rebuilt by ACR 8/91
2003	ACR 202	A4069 (GMD)	1981	Rebuilt by ACR 6/91
2004	ACR 203	A4070 (GMD)	1981	Rebuilt by ACR 3/90
2005	ACR 204	A4071 (GMD)	1981	Rebuilt by ACR 4/91
2006	ACR 205	A4072 (GMD)	1981	Rebuilt by ACR 11/90

GP35m — 2000 Horsepower

WC No.	Former No.	Builder No.	Date	Notes
2053	WC 4005	28929	2/64	Ex-MP 2609, 2519, MP 621, rebuilt back to GP35 by WC, 1995.
4002	MP 2603	28777	1/64	MP 2505, T&P 2505, T&P 605; will be WC 2051.
4004	MP 2608	28790	1/64	Ex-MP 2516, MP 618; will be WC 2052.
4006	MP 2610	28931	2/64	Ex-MP 2521, MP 623; will be WC 2054.
4007	MP 2611	29805	1/65	Ex-MP 2523, MP 625; will be WC 2055.
4008	MP 2612	29813	3/65	Ex-MP 2530, MP 633; will be WC 2056.
4009	MP 2613	29824	3/65	Ex-MP 2541, T&P 2541, T&P 644; will be WC 2057.
4010	MP 2614	29826	4/65	Ex-MP 2543, T&P 2543, T&P 646; will be WC 2058.
4011	MP 2616	29648	9/64	Ex-MP 2560, C&EI 2560, C&EI 663, C&EI 255; will be WC 2059. First unit painted WC colors.
4012	WC 4001	28775	12/63	Ex-MP 2602, MP 2503, T&P 2503, T&P 603; will be WC 2060.
4013	WC 4003	28779	1/64	Ex-MP 2605, 2507, T&P 2507, T&P 607; will be WC 2061.

These units were de-turbocharged in 1974, then rebuilt with 645 power assemblies and upgraded to GP38-2 specifications by MP in 1976-77. All were retired by UP in 1986 and sold to Wilson Railway Equipment Corp., Des Moines, Iowa. WC acquired them from Wilson in 1987. They were painted in original WC colors by Wilson.

SD24 — 2400 Horsepower

WC No.	Former No.	Builder No.	Date	Notes
2401	FRVR 2401	25212	5/59	Ex-SUSA 6255, ex-MMID 6255, ex-BN 6255 (traded in to GE 7/82), nee CB&Q 515; to FRVR 5/89
2402	FRVR 2402	25207	5/59	Ex-SUSA 880 (lettered "Lackawanna"), ex-MMID 6250, ex-BN 6250 (traded in to GE 6/82), nee CB&Q 510; to FRVR 5/89

ALCO RSD15 — 2400 Horsepower

WC No.	Former No.	Builder No.	Date	Notes
2400	FRVR 2400	81764	4/59	Ex-LS&I 2400, AT&SF 9802, nee AT&SF 802, scrapped 1996
2403	FRVR 2403	83054	6/60	Ex-LS&I 2403, AT&SF 9844, nee AT&SF 844, scrapped 1996
2404	GB&W 2404	83469	5/59	Ex-LS&I 2404, AT&SF 9810, nee AT&SF 810, scrapped 1996
2405	GB&W 2405	83574	5/60	Ex-LS&I 2405, AT&SF 9838, nee AT&SF 838, scrapped 1996
2406	GB&W 2406	83466	5/59	Ex-LS&I 2401, AT&SF 9807, nee AT&SF 807, scrapped 1996
2407	GB&W 2407	83577	5/60	Ex-LS&I 2402, AT&SF 9841, nee AT&SF 841, held for preservation

These units were never stenciled or operated by WC.

SD35 — 2500 Horsepower

WC No.	Former No.	Builder No.	Date	Notes
2500	FRVR 2500	30830	10/65	Ex-Sou 3024, retired 3/26/86, to Cycle Systems 2/89, FRVR 5/89, nose chopped

GP35 — 2500 Horsepower

WC No.	Former No.	Builder No.	Date	Notes
723	Soo 723	29480	7/64	Will be WC 2551
724	Soo 724	29481	7/64	Will be WC 2552
726	Soo 726	30129	5/65	Will be WC 2553
731	Soo 731	30134	5/65	Will be WC 2555
2554	WC 728	30131	5/65	Ex-Soo 728
2556	WC 831	28966	4/64	Ex-FRVR, nee C&NW 831
2557	WC 832	28967	4/64	Ex-FRVR, nee C&NW 832
2558	WC 840	28975	4/64	Ex-FRVR, nee C&NW 840
—	FRVR 846	29762	2/65	Ex-C&NW 846, used by FRVR, to WC for parts only; hood and turbocharger used on 2053

GP40/GP40-2 — 3000 Horsepower - Acquired 7/90

WC No.	Former No.	Builder No.	Date	Notes
3000	GWWR 3000	36824	8/70	Ex-CM&W 3000, nee WP 3517, Note 2
3002	GWWR 3002	36826	8/70	Ex-CM&W 3002, nee WP 3519, Note 2
3003	GWWR 3003	36827	8/70	Ex-CM&W 3003, nee WP 3520, Note 2
3004	GWWR 3004	36828	8/70	Ex-CM&W 3004, nee WP 3521, Note 2

3005	GWWR 3005	36783	8/70	Ex-CM&W 3005, nee WP 3522, Note 1
3006	GWWR 3006	36784	8/70	Ex-CM&W 3006, nee WP 3523, Note 1
3007	GWWR 3007	36785	8/70	Ex-CM&W 3007, nee WP 3524, Note 1
3009	GWWR 3009	36787	8/70	Ex-CM&W 3009, nee WP 3526, Note 1
3010	CSX 6843	38568	8/71	Ex-C&O 4088; to WC 10/94
3011	GWWR 3011	37839	9/71	Ex-CM&W 3011, ex-UP 676, nee WP 3528, Note 1
3012	GWWR 3012	37840	9/71	Ex-CM&W 3012, nee WP 3529, Note 2
3014	GWWR 3014	37842	9/71	Ex-CM&W 3014, ex-UP 679, nee WP 3531, Note 1
3015	GWWR 3015	37843	9/71	Ex-CM&W 3015, ex-UP 680, nee WP 3532; named "Ralph C. Bryant," wrecked Green Bay 1/24/95, retired, Note 1
3017	GWWR 3017	37845	9/71	Ex-CM&W 3017, nee WP 3534, Note 2
3018	CSX 6750	35108	1/70	Ex-SBD 6750, nee SCL 1595; to WC 6/94
3021	CSX 6612	38427	10/71	Ex-B&O 4037; to WC 6/94, briefly numbered WC 3001
3022	GWWR 3022	37850	9/71	Ex-CM&W 3022, nee WP 3539, Note 1
3023	GWWR 3023	37852	9/71	Ex-CM&W 3023, nee WP 3541, Note 1
3024	GWWR 3024	37853	9/71	Ex-CM&W 3024, nee WP 3542, Note 2
3025	GWWR 3025	37854	9/71	Ex-CM&W 3025, ex-UP 690, nee WP 3543, Note 2
3026	ACR 190	32300	10/66	Ex-NRE 2018, ex-Soo 2018, ex-MILW 2018:2, nee MILW 192; rebuilt to GP40-2 1994
3027	ACR 191	32478	1/67	Ex-NRE 2034, ex-Soo 2034, ex-MILW 2034, nee MILW 161; rebuilt to GP40-2 1994
—	CSX 6783			Acquired for parts only

1. GP-40s from Gateway Western (former Chicago, Missouri & Western) units rebuilt by WC at North Fond du Lac and Stevens Point.
2. GP-40s from Gateway Western (former Chicago, Missouri & Western) units rebuilt at Livingston Rebuild Center, Livingston, Mont. Road numbers on engineer's side stenciled incorrectly by LRC.

GP7/GP7R — 1500 Horsepower

WC No.	Former No.	Builder No.	Date	Notes
4119	FRVR 4119	15179	10/51	Ex-C&NW 4119, CRI&P 4444, nee 1220, rebuilt 4/75
4133	FRVR 4133	15189	11/51	Ex-C&NW 4133, CRI&P 4458, nee 1230, rebuilt 4/76
4146	FRVR 4146	17077	8/52	Ex-C&NW 4146, CRI&P 4471, first 4483, N&W 3476, nee WAB 476, rebuilt 5/75; to Badger Mining Co., 1995, chop-nosed
4151	FRVR 4151	12939	4/51	Ex-C&NW 4151, CRI&P 4476, first 4493, nee SLSF 547, rebuilt 2/75
4159	FRVR 4159	15182	10/51	Ex-C&NW 4159, CRI&P 4505, nee 1223, rebuilt 2/76
4304	FRVR 4304	22881	3/57	Ex-C&NW 4304, 603, nee M&StL 603; rebuilt 5/72, chop-nosed, to WSOR 6/95
4310	FRVR 4310	18239	5/53	Ex-C&NW 4310, nee 1627, rebuilt 5/72, chop-nosed
4326	FRVR 4326	20685	9/55	Ex-C&NW 4326, nee 1719, rebuilt 4/72, chop-nosed, to WSOR 6/95
4329	FRVR 4329	14294	3/51	Ex-C&NW 4329, nee 1527; rebuilt 12/73 chop-nosed, to WSOR 6/95
4330	FRVR 4330	14295	3/51	Ex-C&NW 4330, nee 1528, rebuilt 12/73, chop-nosed; never ran on WC
4332	FRVR 4332	14300	3/51	Ex-C&NW 4332, nee 1533, rebuilt 11/73, chop-nosed

GP9R — 1750 Horsepower

WC No.	Former No.	Builder No.	Date	Notes
1701	FRVR 1701	24755	9/58	Ex-FRVR 4509, ex-C&NW 4509, 700, nee M&StL 700, rebuilt 1974, chop-nosed
1702	FRVR 1702	23559	9/57	Ex-FRVR 4503, ex-C&NW 4503, nee 1742, rebuilt 11/72, chop-nosed
4501	FRVR 4501	23552	6/57	Ex-C&NW 4501, nee 1735, rebuilt 9/72, chop-nosed
4502	FRVR 4502	22820	11/56	Ex-C&NW 4502, 600, nee M&StL 600, rebuilt 9/72, chop-nosed
4504	FRVR 4504	24763	10/58	Ex-C&NW 4504, 708, nee M&StL 708, rebuilt 10/73, chop-nosed
4505	FRVR 4505	14314	4/51	Ex-C&NW 4505, nee 1547, rebuilt 10/73, chop-nosed
4506	FRVR 4506	24768	10/58	Ex-C&NW 4506, 713, nee M&StL 713, rebuilt 11/73, chop-nosed
4508	FRVR 4508	24765	10/58	Ex-C&NW 4508, 710, nee M&StL 710, rebuilt 1974, chop-nosed
4510	FRVR 4510	24759	10/58	Ex-C&NW 4510, 704, nee M&StL 704, rebuilt 1974, chop-nosed
4514	FRVR 4514	A-1919	5/60	Ex-PNC 177, ex-Bellequip 177, nee QNS&L 177, rebuilt 4/76, high nose

SD40/SD40-2 — 3000 Horsepower

WC No.	Former No.	Builder No.	Date	Notes
6001	ACR 181	A2562 (GMD)	10/71	SD40
6002	ACR 183	A2869 (GMD)	8/73	Rebuilt by ACR 1989
6003	ACR 185	A2871 (GMD)	9/73	Rebuilt by ACR 1989
6004	ACR 186	A2955 (GMD)	9/73	Rebuilt by ACR 1989
6005	ACR 187	A2956 (GMD)	10/73	Rebuilt by ACR 1989
6006	ACR 188	A2957 (GMD)	10/73	Rebuilt by ACR 1989

SD45 — 3450 Horsepower

WC No.	Former No.	Builder No.	Date	Notes
6495	WC 6417	33038	5/67	Ex-BN 6417, nee NP 3617
6496	WC 6494	36796	8/70	Ex-BN 6494, ordered by CB&Q (533) delivered to BN
6497	WC 6660	33022	2/67	Ex-BN 6660, nee SLSF 911
6498 (2nd)	WC 6677	35477	9/69	Ex-BN 6677, nee SLSF 929. First SD45 painted WC colors.
6499 (2nd)	WC 6690	35490	10/69	Ex-BN 6690, nee SLSF 943
6500	WC 6498 (1st)	37106	5/71	Ex-BN 6498
6501 (2nd)	WC 6499 (1st)	37107	5/71	Ex-BN 6499
6502 (2nd)	WC 6501 (1st)	37109	5/71	Ex-BN 6501
6503	WC 6502 (1st)	37110	5/71	Ex-BN 6502
6504	BN 6504	37112	5/71	
6505	BN 6505	37113	5/71	
6506	BN 6506	37114	5/71	
6507	BN 6507	37115	5/71	
6508	BN 6508	37116	5/71	
6509	WC 6510 (1st)	37118	6/71	Ex-BN 6510

6510 (2nd)	WC 6511 (1st)	37119	6/71	Ex-BN 6511
6511 (2nd)	WC 6517 (1st)	37125	6/71	Ex-BN 6517
6512	WC 6522 (1st)	37130	6/71	Ex-BN 6522
6513	WC 6523 (1st)	37131	6/71	Ex-BN 6523, named "Richard J. Ogilvie"
6514	WC 6524 (1st)	37132	6/71	Ex-BN 6524
6515	WC 6526 (1st)	37134	6/71	Ex-BN 6526
6516	WC 6527 (1st)	37135	7/71	Ex-BN 6527
6517	WC 6530 (1st)	37138	7/71	Ex-BN 6530
6518	WC 6531 (1st)	37139	7/71	Ex-BN 6531
6519	WC 6532 (1st)	37140	7/71	Ex-BN 6532
6520	WC 6533 (1st)	37141	7/71	Ex-BN 6533; "Anniversary" unit: FV&W 1st, WC 7th
6521	WC 6534	37142	7/71	Ex-BN 6534
6522 (2nd)	WC 6535	37143	7/71	Ex-BN 6535
6523 (2nd)	WC 6537	37145	8/71	Ex-BN 6537
6524 (2nd)	WC 6538	37146	8/71	Ex-BN 6538
6525	WC 6539	37147	8/71	Ex-BN 6539
6526 (2nd)	WC 6541	37149	8/71	Ex-BN 6541
6527 (2nd)	WC 6543	5794-1	11/71	Ex-BN 6543
6528	WC 6548	5794-6	11/71	Ex-BN 6543
6529	WC 6553 (1st)	5794-11	11/71	Ex-BN 6553
6530 (2nd)	WC 6554 (1st)	5794-12	11/71	Ex-BN 6554
6531 (2nd)	WC 6559	5794-17	12/71	Ex-BN 6559
6532 (2nd)	WC 6560	5794-18	12/71	Ex-BN 6560
6533 (2nd)	WC 6561	38368	10/71	Ex-WC 6572 (1st), ex-BN 6572, nee C&S 870
6655 (1st)	BN 6655	33016	2/67	Ex-SLSF 905; painted for WC first anniversary, retired 12/93, scrapped

SD45 — 3450 Horsepower
Units acquired 1994 from EMD

WC No.	Former No.	Builder No.	Date	Notes
6550	WC 6571	36120	3/70	Ex-EMD 3101, nee Sou second 3101; rebuilt by WC, 8/94
6551	WC 6572 (2nd)	33592	12/67	Ex-EMD 3115, nee Sou 3115; rebuilt by WC, 7/94, named "Customer Minded Employees"
6552	WC 6573	33549	11/67	Ex-EMD 3127, nee Sou 3127; rebuilt by WC, 8/94
6553 (2nd)	WC 6574	33554	11/67	Ex-EMD 3132, nee Sou 3132
6554 (2nd)	WC 6575	33557	11/67	Ex-EMD 3135, nee Sou 3135
6555	WC 6576	33569	11/67	Ex-EMD 3147, nee Sou 3147
6556	WC 6577	33571	11/67	Ex-EMD 3149, nee Sou 3149; rebuilt by WC, 7/94

SD45 — 3450 Horsepower

Acquired 1993 from AT&SF

WC No.	Former No.	Builder No.	Date	Date rebuilt	Notes
6578	AT&SF 5300	32599	12/66	3/80	Ex-AT&SF 5583, nee 1883
6579	AT&SF 5301	32545	12/66	3/80	Ex-AT&SF 5569, nee 1869
6580	AT&SF 5303	32077	8/66	4/80	Ex-AT&SF 5521, nee 1821
6581	AT&SF 5304	32541	12/66	7/81	Ex-AT&SF 5565, nee 1865
6582	AT&SF 5305	32546	12/66	7/81	Ex-AT&SF 5570, nee 1870
6583	AT&SF 5306	32549	12/66	8/81	Ex-AT&SF 5573, nee 1873
6584	AT&SF 5307	32064	6/66	8/81	Ex-AT&SF 5508, nee 1808
6585	AT&SF 5308	32518	11/66	9/81	Ex-AT&SF 5542, nee 1842
6586	AT&SF 5310	32076	8/66	10/81	Ex-AT&SF 5520, nee 1820
6587	AT&SF 5311	32081	8/66	10/81	Ex-AT&SF 5525, nee 1825
6588	AT&SF 5312	32542	12/66	10/81	Ex-AT&SF 5566, nee 1866
6589	AT&SF 5315	32547	12/66	12/81	Ex-AT&SF 5571, nee 1871
6590	AT&SF 5317	32071	6/66	1/82	Ex-AT&SF 5517, nee 1817
6591	AT&SF 5319	32063	6/66	1/82	Ex-AT&SF 5507, nee 1807
6592	AT&SF 5320	32510	10/66	1/82	Ex-AT&SF 5534, nee 1834
6593	AT&SF 5321	32520	11/66	1/82	Ex-AT&SF 5544, nee 1844
6594	AT&SF 5323	32529	11/66	2/82	Ex-AT&SF 5553, nee 1853
6595	AT&SF 5405	32517	11/66	7/85	Ex-AT&SF 5496, 5541, nee 1841
6596	AT&SF 5406	32070	6/66	6/85	Ex-AT&SF 5497, 5515, nee 1815
6597	AT&SF 5407	32506	10/66	4/85	Ex-AT&SF 5498, 5530, nee 1830
6598	AT&SF 5408	32527	11/66	2/85	Ex-AT&SF 5499, 5551, nee 1851
—	AT&SF 5318	32528	11/66	4/79	Ex-AT&SF 5552, nee 1852, acquired for parts

AT&SF 5405-5408 were fitted with Sulzer 16-ASV25/30 prime movers by Morrison Knudsen in 1980 and 1981. They were restored to standard SD45 configuration by AT&SF in 1985 after the conclusion of the test of the Sulzer engines.

Acquired 1994-95 from AT&SF

WC No.	Former No.	Builder No.	Date	Date rebuilt	Notes
6599	AT&SF 5327	32072	6/66	5/82	Ex-AT&SF 5516, nee 1816
6600	AT&SF 5328	32563	12/66	6/82	Ex-AT&SF 5587, nee 1887
6601	AT&SF 5329	32513	10/66	6/82	Ex-AT&SF 5537, nee 1837
6602	AT&SF 5331	32537	12/66	7/82	Ex-AT&SF 5561, nee 1861
6603	AT&SF 5332	32556	12/66	7/82	Ex-AT&SF 5580, nee 1880
6604	AT&SF 5334	32078	8/66	8/82	Ex-AT&SF 5522, nee 1822
6605	AT&SF 5336	32550	12/66	9/82	Ex-AT&SF 5574, nee 1874
6606	AT&SF 5337	32551	12/66	9/82	Ex-AT&SF 5575, nee 1875
6607	AT&SF 5339	32075	12/66	10/82	Ex-AT&SF 5519, nee 1819
6608	AT&SF 5341	32525	11/66	11/82	Ex-AT&SF 5549, nee 1849

6609	AT&SF 5342	32058	6/66	11/82	Ex-AT&SF 5502, nee 1802
6610	AT&SF 5344	32561	12/66	12/82	Ex-AT&SF 5585, nee 1885
6611	AT&SF 5345	32516	10/66	12/82	Ex-AT&SF 5540, nee 1840
6612	AT&SF 5346	32515	12/66	12/82	Ex-AT&SF 5576, nee 1876
6613	AT&SF 5377	36498	6/70	1/84	Ex-AT&SF 5619
6614	AT&SF 5379	36494	6/70	1/84	Ex-AT&SF 5615
6615	AT&SF 5382	35005	6/69	5/85	Ex-AT&SF 5600
6616	AT&SF 5383	34998	4/69	5/85	Ex-AT&SF 5593
6617	AT&SF 5384	35003	5/69	6/85	Ex-AT&SF 5598
6618	AT&SF 5386	34995	4/69	6/85	Ex-AT&SF 5590
6619	AT&SF 5388	34996	4/69	6/85	Ex-AT&SF 5591
6620	AT&SF 5390	36480	5/69	7/85	Ex-AT&SF 5611
6621	AT&SF 5391	35013	5/69	7/85	Ex-AT&SF 5608
6622	AT&SF 5392	35012	5/69	7/85	Ex-AT&SF 5607
6623	AT&SF 5393	35011	5/69	7/85	Ex-AT&SF 5606
6624	AT&SF 5394	35002	4/69	8/85	Ex-AT&SF 5597
6625	AT&SF 5395	35008	5/69	8/85	Ex-AT&SF 5603
6626	AT&SF 5396	35009	5/69	8/85	Ex-AT&SF 5604
6627	AT&SF 5397	35000	4/69	8/85	Ex-AT&SF 5595
6628	AT&SF 5399	35004	5/69	9/85	Ex-AT&SF 5599
6629	AT&SF 5400	34999	4/69	9/85	Ex-AT&SF 5594
6630	AT&SF 5402	35001	4/69	9/85	Ex-AT&SF 5596
6631	AT&SF 5381	35014	5/69	5/85	Ex-AT&SF 5609

F45/FP45 — 3450 Horsepower

WC No.	Former No.	Builder No.	Date	Date rebuilt	Notes
6650	AT&SF 5955	34041	6/68	9/82	Ex-AT&SF 5905, nee 1905
6651	AT&SF 5956	34042	6/68	5/82	Ex-AT&SF 5906, nee 1906
6652	AT&SF 91	33190	12/67	10/82	FP45. Ex-AT&SF 5991, 104, 5941, nee 101
6653	AT&SF 5959	34045	6/68	11/82	Ex-AT&SF 5909, nee 1909
6654	AT&SF 5965	34051	6/68	9/82	Ex-AT&SF 5915, nee 1915
6655 (2nd)	AT&SF 5972	34058	6/68	1/82	Ex-AT&SF 5922, nee 1922
6656	AT&SF 5981	34067	7/68	8/82	Ex-AT&SF 5931, nee 1931

Algoma Central Railway, Inc.

FP9 — 1750 Horsepower

WC No.	Former No.	Builder No.	Date	Notes
1750	VIA 6502	A632	10/54	Ex-CN 6502
1751	VIA 6506	A636	12/54	Ex-CN 6506
1752	VIA 6511	A641	1/55	Ex-CN 6511
1753	VIA 6514	A1044	1/57	Ex-CN 6514
1754	VIA 6525	A1197	4/57	Ex-CN 6525
1755	VIA 6531	A1203	5/57	Ex-CN 6531

FP7Au — 1500 Horsepower

WC No.	Former No.	Builder No.	Date	Notes
1756	VIA 6553	A524	6/53	Ex-VIA 1404, CP 1404, nee 4103

F9B — 1750 Horsepower

WC No.	Former No.	Builder No.	Date	Notes
1760	VIA 6602	A619	10/54	Ex-CN 6602
1761	VIA 6606	A623	12/54	Ex-CN 6606
1762	VIA 6613	A763	2/55	Ex-CN 6613
1763	VIA 6614	A1053	1/57	Ex-CN 6614

Oxford Group, Inc. Locomotives

The Oxford Group, Inc., a locomotive leasing company that involved several WC principals, owned several locomotives that were painted in WC colors or carried WC initials. The following units wore full WC paint: ex-N&W SD45s 1701, 1718, 1724, 1744, 1745-46, and ex-SP SD45s 8939, 8993, 9093. Several other units wore WC initials before being sold. Oxford no longer owns any locomotives.

Abbreviations

ACR	Algoma Central Railway	C&S	Colorado & Southern Railway
AMF	AMF Technotransport, Inc. (rebuilder), Montreal, Que.	CB&Q	Chicago, Burlington & Quincy Railroad
		CRI&P	Chicago, Rock Island & Pacific Railway (Rock Island)
AT&SF	Atchison, Topeka & Santa Fe Railway (Santa Fe)		
Badger	Badger Mining Company, Taylor, Wis.	CR	Consolidated Rail Corporation (Conrail)
B&O	Baltimore & Ohio Railroad	CM&W	Chicago, Missouri & Western
BN	Burlington Northern Railroad Co.	DT&I	Detroit, Toledo & Ironton
CALM	Caddo, Antoine & Little Missouri	EL	Erie-Lackawanna Railroad
CN	Canadian National Railways	FRVR	Fox River Valley Railroad
C&O	Chesapeake & Ohio Railway	GB&W	Green Bay & Western Railroad
C&NW	Chicago & North Western Transportation Co.	GE	General Electric Co.
C&EI	Chicago & Eastern Illinois Railway	GMD	General Motors Diesel Division, London, Ontario

GTW	Grand Trunk Western Railroad, Inc.	NYC	New York Central System
GWWR	Gateway Western Railway	PC	Penn Central
HB&T	Houston Belt & Terminal Railway	PRR	Pennsylvania Railroad
IAIS	Iowa Interstate Railroad, Ltd.	PNC	Precision National Corp.
IHRC	Indiana Hi-Rail Corp.	QNS&L	Quebec North Shore & Labrador Railroad
KB&S	Kankakee, Beaverville & Southern Railroad Company	RDG	Reading Company
KCS	Kansas City Southern Railway	RT&HS	Reading Company Technical & Historical Society
K&IT	Kentucky & Indiana Terminal	SBD	Seaboard System Railroad
KGB&W	Kewaunee, Green Bay & Western Railroad	SCL	Seaboard Coast Line Railroad
L&HR	Lehigh & Hudson River Railway	SLH&TS	Soo Line Historical & Technical Society
LRC	Livingston Rebuild Center, Livingston, Mont.	SLSF	St. Louis-San Francisco Railway (Frisco)
MILW	Chicago, Milwaukee, St. Paul & Pacific Railroad (The Milwaukee Road)	Soo	Soo Line Railroad Company
		Sou	Southern Railway Co.
M&StL	Minneapolis & St. Louis Railway	SP	Southern Pacific
MNNR	Minnesota Commercial Railway	SUSA	Steamtown USA
MMID	Maryland Midland Railway, Inc.	T&P	Texas & Pacific Railway
MP	Missouri Pacific Railroad Co.	UP	Union Pacific Railroad
MT	Minnesota Transfer Railway	VIA	VIA Rail Canada, Inc.
N&W	Norfolk & Western Railway	WAB	Wabash Railroad Co.
NS	Norfolk Southern Corp.	WC	Wisconsin Central Ltd.
NP	Northern Pacific Railway	WP	Western Pacific Railroad Co.

Acknowledgments

Pete Briggs, Jim Fisk, Robert Nadrowski. EMD Product Reference Data, *Extra 2200 South,* Railfan BBS. Robert C. Anderson, Ken Ardinger, Jeff Hampton, Fred Hyde, John Lutz, Joe Lallensack, Nick Modders, Fred H. Worsfold. Special thanks to J. David Ingles.

INDEX

UPDATE

LATE-BREAKING ITEMS

On October 17, 1996, Wisconsin Central Ltd. filed an application with the Surface Transportation Board (the successor to the Interstate Commerce Commission) seeking approval of its purchase from Union Pacific of two lines totaling 18 miles from Hayward to Hayward Junction, Wis., and in the Wausau, Wis., area. The sale was expected to close by the end of 1996.

In a separate transaction, on October 24, 1996, Union Pacific and Wisconsin Central announced that the companies had signed a letter of intent for WC to purchase UP's former Chicago & North Western lines in northern Wisconsin and Upper Michigan. The lines extend from North Green Bay to Ishpeming, Mich.; from Powers to Iron Mountain (Antoine), Mich.; from Quinnesec, Mich., to Niagara, Wis.; and from Cascade to Palmer, Mich. The lines comprise approximately 220 route miles of track.

These lines were isolated from the remainder of the C&NW system after the track south of Green Bay was sold to the Fox River Valley Railroad in 1988. When UP

acquired the C&NW in 1995, it began selling off the remaining isolated ex-C&NW lines.

When the transaction is completed, WC will (together with the Lake Superior & Ishpeming) directly serve the Empire Mine on the Marquette iron ore range. WC will have its own taconite pellet handling facility and dock at Escanaba for transloading pellets into lake boats. WC will also serve several paper mills at Quinnesec, Niagara, and Menominee, Mich.

The new lines will give WC a shorter route from the Marquette area to Escanaba and Gladstone, Mich. Before the sale, Marquette traffic destined for western points first had to move east on the former DSS&A to Trout Lake, Mich., then west to Escanaba. It is likely some former Soo and DSS&A lines will be abandoned as a result of the UP line acquisition.

Consummation of the transaction was expected in late 1996 or early 1997, subject to governmental approvals and final approval of the sale agreement by the boards of directors of both companies.